The Acts of the Apostles

written and illustrated
by
Steven P. Thomason

The Acts of the Apostles

Steven P. Thomason

Published by:

Steve Thomason

www.stevethomason.net

All rights reserved. No part of this book may be reproduced or transmitted in any form or by any means, electronic or mechanical, including photocopying, recording or by any information storage and retrieval system without written permission from the author.

Scripture quotations marked (NIV) are taken from the HOLY BIBLE, NEW INTERNATIONAL VERSION®. NIV®. Copyright© 1973, 1978, 1984 by International Bible Society. Used by permission of Zondervan. All rights reserved.

First printing
Hart Haus Resources, LLC ©2007

reprinted
Steve Thomason © 2016

Special Thanks to:
The Hart Haus Community

Copyright © 2016 Steven P. Thomason

ISBN: 0-9840670-2-7
13-Digit: 978-0-9840670-2-2

Cover Artwork and Interior Illustration: Steven P. Thomason

Printed in the United States of America

Introduction

About This Study

This study was originally written in the spring of 2005 for a network of house churches called Hart Haus. Each week the members of the community would commit to spend 5 days studying the designated passage of scripture and then share what they learned with the group when they gathered in the various homes on Sunday.

Originally, this was designed to be a 12-week study, with 60 daily lessons. You may choose to follow the fast-paced, 12-week study, or you may choose to slow down and spread it out over a longer period of time. To facilitate a more flexible format, this version is structured around **Sessions**, and **Lessons** rather than **Weeks** and ***Days***. Feel free to use whatever method fits best with your group's needs.

About the Author

Steve Thomason is first and foremost a child of God that is committed to loving his wife and four children. He currently resides in the suburbs of Minneapolis, Minnesota.

Steve has two passions in life. The first is teaching people about God and how to grow in a relationship with the Creator. His second passion is art -- specifically cartooning and animation. Throughout his career he has sought to blend these two passions together to create visually interesting lessons that draw people closer to God.

From 1994-2002 Steve was in Adult Minstries at Central Christian Church in Las Vegas, Nevada. During those years Steve led small group ministries, adult education classes, and wrote curriculum for both settings. Along the way he earned a Masters of Divinity degree from Bethel Theological Seminary through their In-Ministry Program.

In 2002 Steve and his family joined with a group of friends to explore what it would look like to "do church" in a different way. For the next 5 years they experimented with being a community in a network of house churches called Hart Haus. During those years Steve wrote a daily Bible Study that combined cartoons and Bible Commentary.

Find more studies and resources at www.stevethomason.net

Acts: The Church is Born

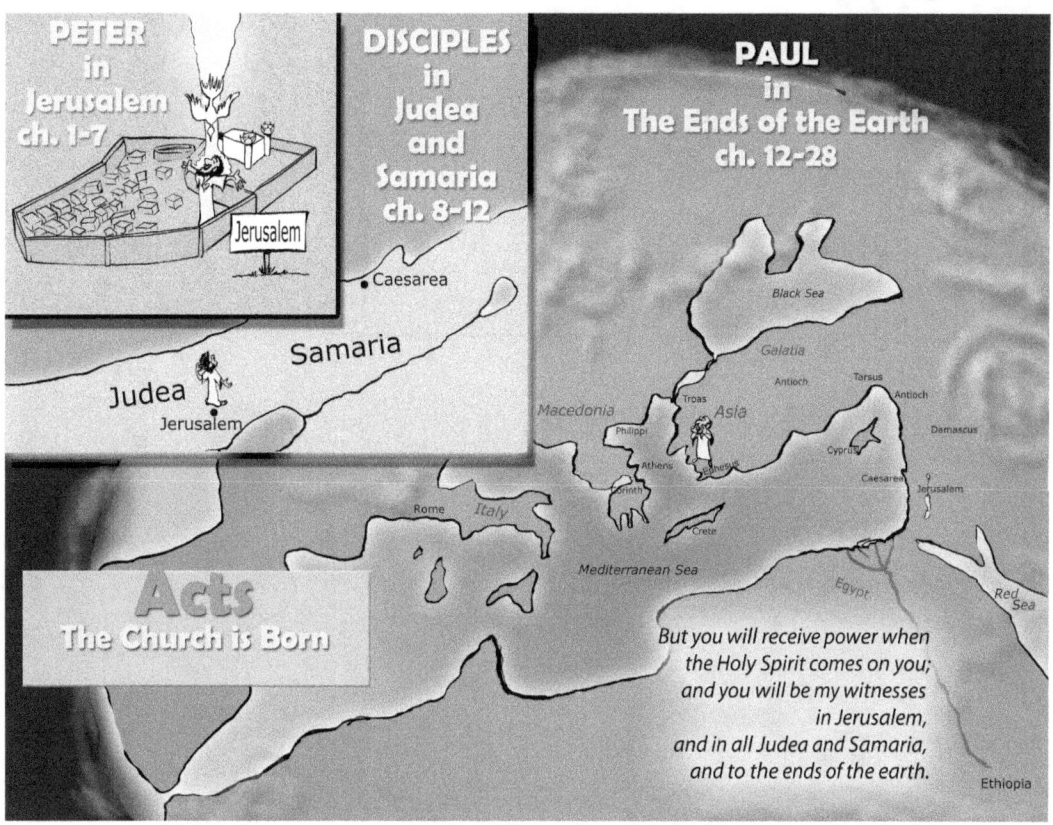

Acts: The Church is Born

Acts: The Church is Born

Session 1: The Church is Planted in Jerusalem

Introduction

If a tree is going to grow strong and tall then it must establish a strong root system. This week, as we study Acts 1-2, we will see the roots of this newly planted church reaching deep into the soil. Jesus is the key to this whole operation. Not only is he the planter of the seed, he is the seed and the soil as well. The church is planted in the truth about who Jesus is and why he came. The disciples were called to be witnesses to the simple, yet profound fact that Jesus conquered sin and death by rising from the dead. They were commanded to take this good news to the entire world.

In order for this sapling church to accomplish the mission for which it was sent, it had to be firmly rooted in three things: Power, Proclamation, and Presence. Without the Power of the Holy Spirit they were nothing; just a sapless, lifeless stick of wood. Without the Proclamation of absolute truth that is found in the person of Jesus Christ there is no mission at all. Only through the life-giving Presence of an authentic community in the world would the love of God and the Good News of Jesus have a vehicle through which to be delivered. We will look at all three of these root structures this week.

Acts: The Church is Born

Session 1: The Church is Planted in Jerusalem

Lesson 1

Acts 1:1-14

What topic did Jesus discuss with his disciples during the time he spent with them following his resurrection? Why?

What are the two kinds of baptism that Jesus contrasts?

What are the similarities and differences between these two baptisms?

What did Jesus promise the disciples would receive?

What were they to do when they received it? Where were they to do this?

Mark these areas on the map provided.

Note: If you don't have a Bible Atlas, you may want to get one. It would be a great addition to your family library. A good one is The Moody Atlas of Bible Lands. Publisher: Moody Publishers (September 1, 1985) ISBN: 0802404383

If you have a Study Bible, it should have a set of maps in the back.

If you don't have an atlas or a good set of maps in your Bible, here are some sites that have reproducible maps. (please note: I am not necessarily endorsing the theology of these sites, but the maps are good!)

http://www.bible.ca/maps

http://www.keyway.ca/htm2002/keyway07.htm

http://www.biblestudy.org/maps/main.html

What promise did the two "Men in White" make about Jesus?

What did the men and women do as they waited for Jesus' gift? Why?

Acts: The Church is Born

Session 1: The Church is Planted in Jerusalem

The Seed is Planted

Inside of a single seed there lies all the genetic information to produce a gigantic living tree. Even more amazing than that is the fact that from that one seed hundreds, even thousands more seeds can be produced. Today Jesus planted the seed of his kingdom into the hearts of his disciples.

The disciples asked him if he was going to restore the Kingdom to Israel at this time. Notice how he did not answer them directly. His silence was like he said, "Hello! Have you not been walking with me and listening to my teaching for the past three years? Yes I'm going to restore the Kingdom, but not in the way that you or all the other Jews think. I am, through you, going to restore the Kingdom of God as it was originally designed...for the whole world. You don't understand this yet, but when the Spirit comes into you on a permanent basis, he will help you discover that you will break the boundaries of race, language, and creed. You will be my witnesses to the entire world.

The seed looks small and unimposing in the beginning. It even lies unseen for a season as it spreads roots. But then, given the proper environment, it bursts forth into a dynamic living organism; the roots of which are strong enough to break up a concrete foundation. As we study the book of Acts we will watch this sprout start tiny with only 120 people, incubate for a while in Jerusalem, and then bust out into the entire world, spreading it's branches for all to see and participate.

Just For Kids

Spend time today getting familiar with the geography of the book of Acts. Use the blank map that was provided in the book. You may want to make some copies of it before you start marking on it. That way you can make a different map for each section of the book. We will be referencing this map throughout the study of Acts, so it would be a good idea to get familiar with it.

Today, read Acts 1:8.

What did Jesus say the disciples would receive when the Holy Spirit filled them?

The Greek word for "power" is dunamos. That's where we get the word "dynamite." In what ways could the power of the Holy Spirit be like dynamite?

Where did Jesus say the disciples should go to be witnesses for him?

Identify the regions where Jesus said to go by marking them on your map. ****Please see the note about maps in the main study.*

Acts: The Church is Born

Session 1: The Church is Planted in Jerusalem

Lesson 2

Acts 1:15-26

Who was Judas and what had he done? (You'll have to review the gospels for this answer)

Peter quoted from Psalm 69 and 109. Read those two Psalms and see if you agree with Peter's interpretation of these two passages.

Who wrote these two Psalms? What relationship did the author have with Jesus? How does (if at all) the meaning of these Psalms change if you hear them spoken from the mouth of Jesus?

What did Peter think needed to be done in regard to Judas' absence? Why?

What method did the disciples use to choose Judas' replacement? Read Proverbs 16:33; Leviticus 16:6-10; Joshua 18:3-10; 1 Chronicles 24:1-5 to see why Peter may have viewed this method as a legitimate way of discerning God's will.

Do you think this is a good method for determining what God's will is in your decision making? Why or why not?

Acts: The Church is Born

Session 1: The Church is Planted in Jerusalem

Life without the Spirit

Scholars have debated long and hard over the correct way to interpret today's passage. Some have said that Peter was operating exactly according to God's design and that it was necessary for a twelfth apostle to be chosen. The number twelve was important because it represented the twelve tribes of Israel. The 12 apostles represented the new Kingdom and the new tribes. If you follow this school of thought, then Peter's method of choosing Matthias by lot was appropriate. After all, it's not like he randomly chose from the crowd. Instead, he and the other apostles prayerfully boiled the selection process down to two equally qualified candidates. At this point they drew from an age old, biblical tradition of casting lots and leaving the ultimate choice in the hands of God, trusting that God would direct the fall of the lots.

While this interpretation is good and can definitely stand, I'd like to explore the possibility of another interpretation. In the flow of the story (tomorrow) we are about to witness one of the greatest miracles of all time. It is the central driving force of the church; the giving of the Holy Spirit. Jesus said that when the Holy Spirit came he would guide the disciples in every step of their mission. In today's reading, perhaps, Luke was giving us a glimpse of what it would look like if the disciples operated without the Holy Spirit. Peter, being the bold and impulsive man that he was, took matters into his own hands, figured out that they needed a replacement, and used "old school" methods to choose one.

Don't blame him; he hadn't received the Holy Spirit yet. He didn't know that Jesus had another man already chosen to fill the role of number twelve; Saul of Tarsus. Of course, at that time Saul was still neck deep in his zealous Pharisaism, so Peter couldn't have possibly seen that one coming. That's just the point. Apart from the Spirit of God, he couldn't have seen it coming. When we move out under our own strength and with our own wisdom, we very seldom make godly choices. Oh, we may make *good* choices (I'm sure Matthias was a top notch guy) but we don't make *God* choices. We so often sacrifice the best on the altar of the good and efficient.

We'll talk more tomorrow about how necessary the Holy Spirit is for us to be able to be all that God wants us to be. Today, simply ask yourself, "Am I listening to the Holy Spirit, or am I closing my eyes and rolling the dice...eenee, meenee, minee, moe?"

Just For Kids

Let's say you and your friends get together and one of the friends has brought his brand new bike. It's the coolest bike you've ever seen. Everyone wants to be the first one to ride it. Obviously, not everyone can be the first one to ride the bike, so how do you decide who gets to go first?

Do you...

a. Allow the owner of the bike to determine who gets to ride first?
b. Not let anyone ride so that there won't be any more fighting
c. Draw straws to see who goes first.

What problems could happen if you chose a?

What problems could happen if you chose b?

Why might c be the best option?

Sometimes, when we have to make big choices, like the disciples had to do, it is OK to "flip a coin" or "draw straws." The truth is that if you are walking with God, God is going to bless you in whichever decision you make, because both options are good ones. God is not as concerned about what you do as God is about how you do what you do and for whom you do it.

STEVE THOMASON
following the cloud

Acts: The Church is Born

Session 1: The Church is Planted in Jerusalem

Lesson 3

Acts 2:1-13

In Deuteronomy 16:1-7, we learn about the three main festivals in the Jewish year. The first is Passover, the second is the Feast of Weeks (Pentecost), and the third is the Feast of Tabernacles.

What did the feast of Passover celebrate?

What key event happened for Christians during the Passover (hint: It was a dark day for Jesus)?

What did the Feast of Weeks (Pentecost) celebrate? (Note: by the 1st century, the Jews had also come to associate Moses' receiving the Law on Mt. Sinai as something to be celebrated at Pentecost in addition to its original purpose)

What key event happened for Christians at the Feast of Weeks in our passage today?

Do you see any correlation between these New Testament events and these Old Testament Feasts? If so, what?

What miraculous event took place when the Holy Spirit came upon the disciples?

Who was represented in the crowd?

Read Genesis 11:5-7 and see if there is any correlation between it and the events in our passage today.

How did the crowd respond to this miracle?

Acts: The Church is Born

Session 1: The Church is Planted in Jerusalem

The Root of Power

The complete title of this book is <u>The Acts of the Apostles</u>. While it definitely records the history of Peter, John, Philip, and Paul, these men are actually secondary characters to the main plotline. Keeping in mind that Acts is the sequel to Luke's Gospel, when we look at both Luke and Acts combined we realize that the unifying character through the story is the Holy Spirit. The Spirit conceived Jesus in Mary's womb. The Spirit anointed Jesus at his baptism and led him into the wilderness to be tempted. The Spirit was the big promise when he went away. We will see as the story unfolds that it is the Spirit that guides (directly, I might add) the activities of the apostles. And, it is that very same Spirit that indwells Jesus' disciples today, eternally connecting us to the never-ending story of Acts. The Holy Spirit is the star of the show. The book should really be called <u>The Acts of the Holy Spirit</u>.

Today we see a promise fulfilled. Jesus said that the disciples would receive power when the Holy Spirit came upon them. The Greek word for power is "dunamos." This is the word from which we get our word "dynamite." Dunamos was an explosive power. It was a driving energy. To carry our tree analogy along, the Holy Spirit is the sap and the life energy that drives a tree to spread its branches and soak in the life giving rays of the sun. Without the Spirit there is no life. Without the Spirit there is no power.

When the Spirit came on them, it blew people away. There was a shaking, a rattling, and a miracle. The crowd at Pentecost had to stand up and pay attention. By the supernatural power of God's Spirit, representatives from every corner of the world instantly heard the truth of Jesus as it was proclaimed in their own language. You might say it was the Spirit's version of a live CNN satellite uplink. From that one moment, the seed of the Kingdom of God was planted into 3,000 lives and was taken back to the far reaches of the world. Most people don't think about this, but because of the miracle at Pentecost, churches were planted all over the world, long before the missionary journeys of Paul, and completely under the leadership of the Holy Spirit and no one else. That is a miracle!

We could spend days, weeks, and months discussing the topic of the Holy Spirit. We could debate over whether tongues was a miracle of speaking in foreign languages or of hearing a foreign language in your mother tongue. We could debate whether tongues is a gift that everyone should receive or if it is only for a few, like all the other gifts. We could debate whether miracles like that can still happen today. We could discuss it, and I'm sure you will discuss it in your house church. You should in fact, spend a great deal of time in your studies in the future researching that subject.

Today, we aren't going to discuss those typical debates. Today we are going to look at one simple fact. When the Spirit is present, there is power. When the Spirit of God is present, the authority of God is present and the beacon of God's truth is present. In an act of unprecedented grace, God Almighty poured out God's powerful Spirit into the hearts of all believers. When the Spirit of God is flowing fully, then there is power. There is power to speak the truth without fear. There is power to heal the sick. There is power to restore sight to the blind. There is power to rescue people from the bondage of darkness, to be cleansed from the filth of sin, and to be transformed into the glorious image of Jesus. Here's the question...when was the last time you felt the power? I'm not talking about a big show. I'm not talking about a power trip where you stand up and everybody marvels at how spiritual you are in public. I'm talking about the real power of God that solidifies your faith and allows you to boldly, yet humbly, surrender to the will of God and the leading of the Holy Spirit. It is the power that allows you to face any obstacle with peace, and more importantly with love. It is the power that allows you to know joy in the midst of any and all circumstances.

Have you tasted that power lately? Here's a bold statement: If we, as a community, are not filled with that power, then we will never be more than a fearful, weak, and benign entity that shines dimly and makes little impact. As we go through this study, ask God to open your heart to the power of the Holy Spirit and discover what that looks like in our day, in our city, right now.

Acts: The Church is Born

Session 1: The Church is Planted in Jerusalem

Just For Kids

Today is another map day! Look at Acts 2:9-11. Find and label all the places on your map that were represented on the day of Pentecost.

How would you have felt if you were one of the people in the crowd at Pentecost and heard a common man from Galilee stand up and speak in your language? Would you have been more likely to listen to what he had to say?

Read Genesis 11:5-7. Why did God do this to the people of Babel?

In our story today, we see that God was, once again, calling all people back to God's self from every part of the world. God wants everyone, from every nation and every language to love him. Maybe be you could be one of the people who takes the good news about Jesus to a nation and a language that has never heard of him before.

Acts: The Church is Born

Session 1: The Church is Planted in Jerusalem

Lesson 4

Acts 2:14-41

Peter believed that the miraculous event that had just taken place was the fulfillment of the prophecy made by Joel centuries earlier. When Joel spoke these words during the reign of King Joash (2 Kings 11-13), the kingdom of Judah had just been devastated by a killer swarm of locusts. They lost everything. Joel warned the people that this devastation had been a punishment for sin and that if they did not repent, a worse devastation could hit the city (which it ultimately did). However, in the fashion of the prophets, Joel paints a picture of hope and what it will be like when the Kingdom of God finally comes on the earth in Joel 2:28-32.

In what ways was this prophecy fulfilled on the day of Pentecost in our reading?

In vv. 22-36, Peter gives the first Christian sermon ever preached. In these verses he spells out to the Jerusalemites who Jesus really is. Make a list of all the important points he makes about the nature and position of Jesus. (If you need a little help, check out the "Just for Kids" section!)

Is it important to believe all of these things about Jesus? Why?

How did the people respond to Peter's message?

What did Peter say needed to be done in response to being confronted with the reality of Jesus?

What did he say would happen if the people did this?

What did Peter plead for the people to do? Why?

Acts: The Church is Born

Session 1: The Church is Planted in Jerusalem

The Root of Proclamation

Yesterday we talked about power. Power is a funny thing. Power is intoxicating. It comes in many forms. There is an old saying, "power corrupts and absolute power corrupts absolutely." Raw power is a destructive force. It is like a wildfire that rages through a neighborhood, devouring everything in its path.

Is that the kind of power that the Holy Spirit brings? Of course not. The power of the Holy Spirit is a focused power, like a LASER beam. The focusing mechanism of the power is found in today's reading. It is found in the Proclamation of the Truth.

When the initial shock wave of the Spirit's outpouring began to diminish, the crowd was left absolutely stunned, and not a little bit confused.

What just happened? Did we imagine it? Who can make any sense out of this?

Peter, now under the leadership of the Holy Spirit, stood up and brought order to the chaos. He brought focus to the power. How? He boldly proclaimed the truth about Jesus. Here lies the second root for the church. We are not bringing an ambiguous and innocuous message about generic, universal love, saying, "Why can't we just all get along." We aren't propagating a power that is akin to harnessing the elemental powers or "life-energy" of the cosmos. We are witnesses to the objective, historical, person of Jesus Christ. He was born, he lived a real life, he died a real death, he rose in bodily form, and he is exalted to the right hand of the Father as the Supreme Lord of the universe. That is our message. That is a message that divides families. It polarizes a crowd. You either believe it, or you don't. This is the message of the Kingdom of God. It is only through the power of the Holy Spirit that we can have the courage to proclaim this message. And, when we cease to proclaim this message, then we no longer will be operating in the power of the Holy Spirit.

There are two questions we must ask today.

1. Do you fully understand who Jesus really is and what he came to do?
2. Can you clearly articulate the message of Jesus, in its Acts 2, unfiltered state, to your culture?

If you answered no to either of these questions, then a top priority for you should be to revisit the Gospels and make sure that you know who it is that you are serving.

Jesus said that there would be many who claim that they served him and called him Lord, but he will respond, "Depart from me, for I never knew you."

We live in the Kingdom of God. The question is whether or not we have entered into the correct Kingdom or an imposter. These are sobering words, but words that need to be pondered nonetheless.

Just For Kids

Who is Jesus? How do you know?

Look at these verses and make a list that describes who Jesus is.

v. 22 Jesus was a _____.

v. 23 Jesus was put to _____.

v. 24 God _____ Jesus from the _____.

v. 33 He was _____ to the _____ _____ of God.

v. 33 He has both received and given the _____ _____.

v. 36 He is both _____ and _____.

If all these things are true about Jesus, and you were one of the people who had just nailed him to the cross a few weeks earlier, how would you be feeling right about now?

Peter said that if you want to make things right with God, then you need to repent and be baptized. Have you been baptized yet? If so, how has your life been different since then? If not, why?

Acts: The Church is Born

Session 1: The Church is Planted in Jerusalem

Lesson 5

Acts 2:42-47

Make a list of the things to which the disciples were devoted. Try to describe what each of these things is.

How did the members of that church treat one another?

How often did they meet together?

Where did they meet? What did they do in each place?

How did the "neighborhood" respond to this church?

What was the result of their presence in the "neighborhood?"

If the description of this first church is to be considered a model for what the church should be like, how well do you think your church is doing in each area?

Rank it from 1-6, 1 being poor and 6 being great, in the following areas:

____ Devoted to apostles' teaching (today, found in Scripture)

____ Devoted to fellowship

____ Devoted to breaking bread

____ Devoted to prayer

____ In awe of God's miracles

____ Sharing everything in common

____ Giving to the needy

____ Meeting daily in the Temple Courts

____ Eating together in their homes with gladness and sincerity

____ Praising God

____ Enjoying the favor of the people

How could you improve in these areas?

Acts: The Church is Born

Session 1: The Church is Planted in Jerusalem

The Root of Presence

Today we see the third root that is necessary for the young tree to grow strong and tall. This root brings balance, for without it the first two roots of Power and Proclamation could become a force in the world that brings nothing but devastation in its wake. Truth always needs to be delivered in the package of Absolute Love. That is what the root of Presence provides. The Kingdom of God is designed to be delivered through the conduit of an authentic, Spirit-filled, God-loving, community. In an authentic community the love of God can be fully demonstrated in real-life and the light of the Gospel can shine through to the world in vivid color. The truth moves from the abstract to the concrete as the power and the truth and the love of God moves in and through the lives of God's people as they interact with one another and with the world around them. The church becomes a Presence within the world that acts as the Salt and the Light that Jesus referred to in Matthew 5.

The key to this is the word authentic. The church must be real, not manufactured. We live in a society that has become an expert at manufacturing artificial reality. If you go to Disneyland you can walk through simulated environments that are so real that when you actually take your children to the real thing in nature they say, "Hey, this is just like Disneyland." We put hardwood floors in our homes that aren't made out of wood. We paint faux finishes on our walls. We put artificial sweeteners in our instant coffee. And, most ironically, we make food products out of bleached flour and plastic.

When we substitute the real ingredients with artificial substances and then package it as the "real thing," do you know what happens? First of all, millions of people slip into a state of ignorant bliss and fill their bodies with harmful toxins, unaware. Secondly, an entire generation slowly dies of malnutrition and the subsequent diseases that accompany the plight of full stomachs and starving cells.

When we apply this principle to the church, the same is true. Here are five ingredients from today's reading that should be present in the church along with the five artificial substitutes that we have settled for. As with baking, when one ingredient is missing from the recipe then the food doesn't taste quite right.

Devotion vs. Distraction

The word devotion (proskartereio) means a. "to focus on," b. "to hold fast to," and c. "to be in continually." It is a matter of priorities. What is first in our lives? Jesus said in Matthew 6:33 that we are to seek first the Kingdom of Heaven and all these things will be added unto you. In our world the areas of the Apostles teaching, Fellowship, Breaking of Bread, and Prayer are things that are most often an addendum to our agenda and under the "optional" or "if I have extra time" category in our weekly maelstrom of activity. We are the people of distraction. Our work, our worries, and our amusement swirl around us and vie for our attention. Who do you think is behind the machine that fills the airwaves with distracting messages? It's not God. Our enemy knows that as long as he can keep us distracted from the things that actually matter in life (eternal life, remember) then he can keep us from adding the most important ingredient to our Presence, leaving us as unsavory salt, and lackluster light in the world.

Wonder vs. Wonder Bread

We talked about this on Lesson 3. The real catalyst for the church is the Power of the Holy Spirit at work in its people. Every day the people were in awe of the miraculous wonders that the Spirit was doing. If we want the dough to rise, then we have to add the yeast. It's like the difference between Wonderbread and Ezekiel bread. Wonderbread may look like bread, but it has been stripped of everything nutritional that God designed wheat to provide. Wonderbread will last for weeks on the shelf because it is so worthless that not even mold wants to eat it. Ezekiel bread, on the other hand, is made with the whole, sprouted grain and is rich with life-giving nutrients. Without the power of God in the church, we have nothing more than bleached flour with no nutritional value. It looks good on the shelf and it can fill your stomach, but it does nothing for your body. When people observe our community, do they see a nicely packaged presentation that looks like bread, but has no actual wheat left in it? Or, do they see bread that is alive with the whole grain goodness of the power of the Spirit of God coursing through it as a regular and expected reality?

Generosity vs. General Apathy

They shared everything in common and gave to anyone as he had need. In our society we have become so desensitized and calloused by the parade of charlatans that have used us over the years that we no longer trust. Or, we have become immobilized by our exposure to the global reality of hunger and poverty that we feel incapable of making any difference in the

Acts: The Church is Born

Session 1: The Church is Planted in Jerusalem

world, and so freeze into inactivity. We horde our finances and resources and rationalize it under the guise of "good stewardship." Until the floodgates of generosity open up in the community, first between the members of the community, and then to the world around it, the practical demonstration of God's love will not be evident to the world. We will have faith without deeds. We will speak hollow words while we turn people out into the cold.

Interdependence vs. Independence

The Great American myth is the belief that we are free agents in the world. Our radical individualism is the destructive factor that dismantles the cohesion necessary to bring unity and to bond us together as the body of Christ. No one person and no one family can be the church. We are part of the body and we need each other to be complete. We must rely upon one another. The reason we don't do this is because, quite frankly, it is scary. To trust is to risk. It requires vulnerability. When we become vulnerable we can be taken advantage of and hurt by people who do not have the same values, or are struggling with their own sin. Yet, if we keep our guards up in order to protect ourselves, we will actually find ourselves locked in the prison of self, disconnected from the body of Christ which is the only source of support we have. If the church is to be a vital Presence in the world, then it must be a cohesive unit that trusts and depends upon one another.

Open System vs. Closed System

The Lord added daily to their numbers those who were being saved. Do you know what that means? It means the church was in a constant state of change. Change! One of the greatest reasons for the demise of the American church is the fear of change. We can slip into the attitude that we really like the few people in our little network and we don't want to lose the fellowship that we have. The realm of biology has taught us that a system that is not open to receive outside influence is a system that will soon die. A healthy system, like a living cell, for instance, has a good balance between internal cohesion and external openness. The outer wall of cell is what is called a semi-permeable membrane. It is strong enough to hold the components of the cell together, but pliable enough to allow outside substances into it for nutrition. The church must become a healthy cell that has a strong cohesion, but also has an open attitude to allow new people to constantly be brought into the fold and made to be a viable member of the body.

Remember, the church in this passage did not set out to add numbers. They simply devoted themselves to the essentials of BEING the Presence and God added the numbers. The church is called to die to itself and all the artificial substitutes that threaten it, be filled with the power of the Holy Spirit, and then be ready to receive the fruit of the overflow that God will bring to it as a result of being real.

The question we must ask ourselves every day is this. What are we baking? Do we have all the ingredients that it takes to be the church, or are we substituting them with artificial substances. Are we serving up Wonderbread or are we the real thing?

Just For Kids

When you hear the word "church" what comes to your mind? Is it a building? Is it a person? What does it look like?

Our passage today describes what the very first church looked like? Is this description the same as what your first thoughts about church were? Why or why not?

What does the word "Fellowship" mean? Get a dictionary and look up the word. The English definition is very similar to the Greek word, which is "Koinonia."

Based on this definition, how good is your fellowship at church right now? What kind of things would need to happen for your fellowship to get better?

Acts: The Church is Born

Acts: The Church is Born

Session 2: Growing Strong in Jerusalem

Introduction

As we are studying the book of Acts, we are drawing an analogy to the growth cycle of a tree. When a seed is planted it is very vulnerable. Birds could come and snatch it up. Rocky soil or weeds could choke it out and kill it. If the tree is going to survive, it must be nurtured and have the proper environment so that it can set its roots and grow strong.

Perhaps you have seen a sapling that is tethered to a pole or to guide wires in order to keep it safe against the wind. Landscape experts will tell you that it is actually dangerous to keep these guides on a tree for too long. The young tree requires exposure to strong winds to be able build up resistance. When it is young, thin, and flexible it will bend in the wind, and in the bending will become strong. Eventually it will grow so thick that the wind will not even affect it. If the guides are kept on the sapling for too long it will become brittle, and when the wind blows, the trunk will break instead of bend.

Think about this statement for a moment: New Growth requires support, Mature Growth requires resistance.

Last week we saw the young sapling of the church setting its roots. God allowed the church to experience favor with all the people for a season. They set their roots in the Power of the Spirit, the Proclamation of the Name of Jesus, and the Presence of an authentic community. This week the guide wires have been taken off and the winds begin to blow. Throughout its history, the church has been barraged with wave upon wave of persecution and resistance. In Acts 3-5 we witness the first of these waves. It is not very strong. It is just enough to wake up the community to reality, and deepen their faith.

Acts: The Church is Born
Session 2: Growing Strong in Jerusalem

Lesson 1

Acts 3

What did the crippled man expect to get from Peter and John?

What did he get instead?

How did this event affect the crowd in Jerusalem?

Create an outline of Peter's message in vv. 12-26.

What was the key to the man's healing?

What would happen if the people repented?

What connection is there between Jesus and the promise God made to Abraham?

Power

A wonderful and amazing event happened in this passage. The name of Jesus healed a man that had been born a cripple. Peter and John didn't have any money to give him, but what they did have blew him away. They had the healing and transforming power of God coursing through them. When he encountered this power he was changed physically, spiritually, and emotionally.

We said that this event was "wonderful" and "amazing." What do those words really mean? In our culture we use these terms loosely. When we step off of a roller coaster we say that it was amazing. When we see a nice movie we hail it as "wonderful." Yet, is that really what the words meant in the 1st century? Verse 10 says that when the people saw the healed man they were filled with "wonder" and "amazement."

The word "wonder" is the Greek word "thambos" and has the sense of being filled with awe to the point of trembling and fear. Interestingly, in Mark 10:32ff, after Jesus had just laid out the harsh truth to the rich young man, the disciples experienced "thambos" at his teaching. The band of disciples sobered up as Jesus spelled out his intense plan of self-sacrifice to them. In the Biblical sense, to be "wonderful" does not mean to be warm and fuzzy and make us feel comfortable. It means to be full of things that are so beyond our comprehension that we are full of awe and wonder in the face of their reality.

The word "amazement" is the translation of the Greek word "ekstasis." This word might sound familiar. From it we get the word "ecstatic." When someone is ecstatic they are "out of their mind." Sometimes, in the Greek world, it was actually used to describe a person who was, indeed, insane – or out of their mind. In other cases, however, the same word is used to describe people who had "supra-rational" spiritual experiences in which they were "out of their mind." In other words, they were caught up into a state of consciousness that was obviously beyond their own rational ability and was obviously coming from an external source. When Peter saw his vision in Acts 10 he was in an ecstatic state ("trance" in the NIV is translating "ekstasis") When Paul was praying in Acts 22, he was in a similar ecstatic state when the Lord spoke to him and told him to leave the city. When the people of Jerusalem witnessed this healing they became ecstatic.

Based upon these definitions we must conclude that saying the people were filled with wonder and amazement does not mean that they said,

Acts: The Church is Born

Session 2: Growing Strong in Jerusalem

"Wow, that was really cool...I wonder if the concession stand is still open." No. They were deeply moved to the point of being changed. They had encountered the mighty power of the Almighty God. They had touched the hem of the garment of grace, and in the touching they were changed.

How often do we experience the wonder of God in our lives?

Purpose

The miraculous healing opened a door for Peter to, once again, proclaim the Gospel to the citizens of Jerusalem. It is important to note the significant role that this message plays in the story line of Acts. Chapters 3-5 parallel the ministry of Jesus, and especially the early part of his ministry. Jesus first came to present the Kingdom of God to the Jews for they were the rightful inheritors of the Kingdom. Centuries before, God had promised Abraham that God would use Abraham's family to be the conduit of blessing for the entire world. The leaders of Jerusalem officially rejected Jesus' offer. Now, Peter, being the representative of the God of second chances, is, once again, offering the Kingdom of God to the Jews. He reminded them (v. 25) that they were the heirs to the promise. That promise was fulfilled in Jesus, and through him the Kingdom of God has been established on the Earth. All they need to do is repent of their lack of faith, be baptized into the new order, and they will enter into his Kingdom.

As is the case whenever the clean and clear truth is boldly proclaimed, the city was polarized. Many flocked to the light of this truth. Others, however, were hardened and began to plot against the church, just as they had plotted against Jesus.

Just For Kids

Let's do an experiment. Tie your shoelaces together and try to walk across the room. Is it hard?

Now imagine what it must have felt like to have had crippled legs for your entire life. How must the man in the story have felt about himself? How do you think he felt about God?

Now, try to imagine how he must have felt when he was instantly able to walk.

In v. 16, what did Peter say was the key to this man's healing?

Do you believe that Jesus is powerful enough to do something wonderful like that today? Why or why not?

Acts: The Church is Born

Session 2: Growing Strong in Jerusalem

Lesson 2

Acts 4:1-22

Who came up to Peter and John?

**Please note that these three groups all share a common bond in the Temple. For them, the rituals of sacrifice and temple worship were the center of their understanding of God.

Read Luke 20:27 to find an important fact about these people. How does this fact impact their view of Peter's message about Jesus?

Why were they upset with Peter and John? (v. 2)

In vv. 8-12 we read Peter's third great message of the Gospel. As he presents the truth to the leaders in Jerusalem, he quotes Psalm 118:22. Read the following verses and try to discover the meaning of the "stone" in this message.

    Isaiah 28:16

    Zechariah 3:9

    Matthew 21:42-44

    1 Peter 2:6-8

    Romans 9:33

How did the leaders respond to Peter and John? What did they tell them to do (or not to do)? Why?

What was Peter's and John's response to the leaders' instructions? Why?

We Can't Help It!

Let's zone in on one simple phrase that is found in v. 20.

"For we cannot help speaking about what we have seen and heard."

Have you ever wondered why many Christians, perhaps even you, struggle with being afraid to share your faith or to speak boldly about Jesus to people who do not know him? There are many reasons, and it would not be fair to paint with too broad a brush on this topic. However, let's just entertain one possibility for a moment. Perhaps we are fearful and timid in our witness because we simply have never really experienced anything worth talking about. Or, the experience of life change that we had when we first came to Jesus has faded from our memory, leaving us with nothing more than a lifeless set of ideas that sit dormant in our soul. For many of us our faith is more of a notion that makes sense to our minds, or is a tradition that feels comfortable to us, than it is a reality that has a dynamic, transforming impact in our daily lives.

For example, perhaps you have experienced something like this: There is a movie that you've heard people talk about. The reports have been that it is a great movie that will impact you deeply. When you hear the reports you may be intrigued, or even excited, but it is not real. You may tell people about this movie you've heard about, but the conversation will be casual. Then, one day, you get a chance to see the movie for yourself. During the viewing your heart is gripped and your adrenaline starts flying. When you exit the theatre, things are different. If you truly believed it was a great movie, then the next time you talk about it you will be a different person. You will be passionate about how great it is and be able to give descriptions of your favorite scenes. Your enthusiasm may inspire someone else to see the movie. What is different? You've experienced it, it changed you, and you can't help but to talk about it. It is now a part of who you are.

While discussing a movie is a weak analogy that pales in comparison to the story of the apostles, the point is still valid. The reason Peter and the others were able to stand before their accusers and defy their threats was simple. They hadn't been coached by an evangelism trainer. They hadn't received a degree in theology. They had simply been transformed by the power of God. It was real to them and they couldn't help but to talk about it.

Acts: The Church is Born

Session 2: Growing Strong in Jerusalem

Today, perhaps you could spend some time praying and asking God to show God's power in your life in a way that makes it real for you. Or, perhaps you could ask God to help you see the power that is at work in and through you that you are not recognizing as the hand of God.

If our church is full of the life-changing power of God, then we won't be able to help but to tell everyone about it. When that happens we might find that people start bringing their sick and crippled to us to experience the same power in their lives. Prepare yourself to be used by God.

Just For Kids

What does it mean to be rejected? Have you ever been rejected by someone? What did that feel like? Why?

Look up the word "capstone." What does it mean? What part does it play in a building?

Do you remember the story of the ugly duckling? When he was a baby chick, he was rejected by his brothers and sisters. He was ridiculed and told that he would amount to nothing. In the end, what happened?

Jesus' story is something like that. In our reading today, we could say it is the story of the ugly stone, instead of the ugly duckling. The people of Israel rejected Jesus and didn't think he fit anywhere in the Kingdom of God. In the end, it turns out that he not only fit in, but was the actual capstone of the Kingdom.

Spend some time memorizing Acts 2:12, "Salvation is found in no one else, for there is no other name under heaven given to men by which we must be saved." This is a very important verse to know about the importance that Jesus plays in the world.

Perhaps you could write the verse out on the board, say it out loud together a few times, and then start erasing one or two words at a time until you can say the whole verse with no helps.

Acts: The Church is Born
Session 2: Growing Strong in Jerusalem

Lesson 3

Acts 4:23-35

What attitude did the disciples have toward God in v. 24?

What question did David ask in vv. 25-26 (Read Psalm 2 for the full context)? Why? How would you describe his emotions in this question?

Who appointed the enemies of Jesus to conspire against him? (vv. 27-28)

What did the disciples ask God to do for them? (vv. 29-30)

Question to ponder: in v. 31, why was there a shaking and a filling? Weren't they already filled in Acts 2? What are some possible explanations for this?

Vv. 32-35 form the second "portrait" of the first church. Compare this passage with Acts 2:42-47. What is similar? What is different? What is the main attribute of this community that stands out in your mind? Why?

Powerful Prayer

When the disciples walked with Jesus, they asked if he would teach them how to pray. The model prayer that he gave them is found in Matthew 6. The basic outline of the prayer is this:

> Father, you are the Almighty, and I'm not.
>
> It is your Kingdom, help me to get in step with you.
>
> Give me my daily bread
>
> Keep me from evil.

In today's reading, we see the first example of the disciples praying this prayer in a real life circumstance. The church had just experienced their wave of resistance. The religious leaders, their spiritual fathers, had rejected them, accused them of being God-haters, and threatened them with harm if they did not cease and desist. Imagine the emotional turmoil they must have felt in the wake of this rejection. Most of us cannot grasp the level of the seismic shock they were experiencing in the fabric of their worldview. They thought they were serving God, yet the people who claimed to be God's representatives told them they were evil. To say the least, they were confused and were most probably struggling with fear and doubt.

Notice what happens, though. They pray. In their prayer they follow the pattern of the master. In this prayer we can learn three important attitudes that we should have in the face of difficult circumstances.

It's God's Kingdom, not ours

They addressed God as Sovereign Lord. He is the creator of all things. We must never forget that nothing is too big for God. Nothing takes God by surprise. God doesn't sit way off in Heaven and think, "Whoa, I didn't see that one coming...now what am I going to do?" No matter how terrible things may get – crucifying your leader, arresting and beating your pastor, losing your job, suffering injustice, etc. – God is actively involved in this world to fulfill God's promise to make all things new.

It's OK to emote to God

They quoted the greatest whiner in the Bible; David. Sometimes we can get this notion that good Christians don't experience fear and doubt. Of course we do, we are human beings. The goal is not to be devoid of emotion like some kind of Vulcan guru. Rather, the goal is to follow the example of David; the man after God's own

Acts: The Church is Born

Session 2: Growing Strong in Jerusalem

heart. David was not afraid to openly express his fear, doubt, confusion, and anger to God. He also wasn't afraid to express it in the forum of his community. After all, we read his heart-journal every time we open the Psalms. Yet, what is different about David as opposed to the average Joe is that David didn't vent for the sake of venting. David brought his emotions to God, authentically expressed them, and then allowed God's truth to pour in, flush them out, and leave him with a sense of peace and perspective at the end of the cathartic process. Just study David's Psalms for a while and you will see that pattern emerge.

The disciples did the same thing. They were confused about the resistance they were experiencing and they expressed their emotion to God. Then they allowed God to deliver them from the fear and confusion and replace it with peace, joy, and perspective.

It's God's work, not our strength

Once they were recalibrated to the promise and perspective of God (thy Kingdom come, thy will be done) then they were able to ask for the proper things. They didn't ask for vengeance. They didn't ask for God to remove their obstacles. They simply asked that God would empower them to be courageous conduits of the work that God wanted to do through them. It isn't about us. It isn't about our ability to strategically map out a plan to overthrow the enemy and rescue souls. It is simply about surrendering to the will of God and not allowing fear to inhibit us from being the conduit of God's power through our lives.

A Booster Shot

Notice what happens after they pray. They experience another, mini, Day of Pentecost experience. The room shook and they were filled with the Spirit. Why did this happen? Hadn't they already received the Spirit? Had they lost the Spirit? People will debate the answer to those questions.

Here is one thought: Perhaps this experience was God's way of saying, "Don't worry guys, I'm still with you. You may have been afraid, and you may have been confused, but you passed the first test with flying colors. Here's a little encouragement and a turbo booster to keep you going."

Just For Kids

Note to parents: Before you read this to the kids, be sure to get set up before hand.

Find your favorite, parent-approved snack. Make sure there is enough for everyone.

Before you pass out the snack randomly choose (flip a coin or something like that) 25-30% of your kids who will not receive any snacks at the time you pass out the snack. When you first say that it is time to pass them out, don't give any to those kids who were chosen. See what the reactions are and be ready to teach to them!

It's snack time at Bible Study!! Let's pass out some snacks before we read the lesson.

Read Acts 4:32-35. What were the people in that church like? How did they treat each other?

When the snacks were passed out how did the kids who got some feel? How did the kids who didn't get any feel?

According to our passage, what should you do about the fact that some kids have a snack and the others don't? Why?

Do you see any ways in your church where some people are in need and others have too much? Think of ways that your church could learn to be better about sharing.

Acts: The Church is Born
Session 2: Growing Strong in Jerusalem

Lesson 4

Acts 4:36-5:11

Was it required for Annanias and Sapphira to sell their possessions and give it to the collective fund?

What, then, was the actual offense that Annanias and Sapphira committed? Why was this so bad?

Who was the instigator behind this act?

To whom did they lie?

Read Deuteronomy 6:13-25 *(The incident at Massah is when the Israelites whined about not having anything to drink in Exodus 16)* Do you see a correlation between the story of Annanias and Sapphira with the children of Israel under Moses' leadership? Is so, what?

What effects did this incident have on the church in Jerusalem? Do you see this as a positive or negative thing? Why?

What are some ways in which we could get tempted to "test the Spirit" in our own lives?

How could we guard against this?

Holy Spirit

Within this story is nestled a significant theological truth. The Holy Spirit is God. Throughout the Bible there is evidence that God exists as the Father, the Son, and the Holy Spirit. Many Christians (and opponents of the Christian faith) have argued over whether the Holy Spirit is a separate person like the Father and the Son, or if the Spirit is simply the "energy" that emanates from the Father and the Son. This passage shows us two important points about the identity of the Holy Spirit.

1. **The Spirit is a person.** You can't lie to an energy emanation. Yet, Annanias and Sapphira lied to the Holy Spirit. The Holy Spirit is a personality with which we can have a relationship.

2. **The Spirit is God.** Notice that Peter interchanges the words. He said that Annanias and Sapphira lied to the Holy Spirit, and in so doing they lied to God.

So, what difference does the knowledge of this make in our lives? It is vital for us to realize that the conduit of intimate relationship with God is the Holy Spirit in our lives. The Father is the Almighty "other than" aspect of God. In His presence we can only tremble and fall on our faces. He loves us, but he is "out there." The Son is no longer physically present on the Earth. We can't know him like the disciples did. It is the Holy Spirit that is our intimate ally the dwells within our own Spirit. We are one with God (Father, Son, and Holy Spirit) because we have the interface with the Spirit. Someday we will be fully united with the fullness of God, but for now we have our intimacy with the Spirit. Praise the Father, that because of God'd love for us, and through the sacrificial work of the Son, and the power of God's name, we have been given the person of the Holy Spirit to live with us and walk with us in every moment of our human experience. Just soak and marvel in that today.

Holy Fear

When a parent trains a small child, there is a certain amount of pain involved. The pain exists on both sides of the equation. Here's how it works. Out of love the parent establishes boundaries to protect the child from foolishness. Out of pride and ignorance the child pushes the boundaries. Out of love the parent inflicts pain into the child's life to reinforce the boundaries. In the inflicting of pain, the parent feels pain because nobody likes pain. Unfortunately, a small child is not mature enough to understand logical arguments for the establishment of

Acts: The Church is Born

Session 2: Growing Strong in Jerusalem

healthy boundaries and can only understand the concrete language of pain.

We can see this parenting pattern throughout the history of God's parenting techniques as God raised up God's child called the Nation of Israel. When God established the Law in the Old Testament for the infant nation, God enforced it quickly and severely with catastrophic events. From our perspective it may seem like God is an evil ogre who only wants to hurt people and steal their fun. (What kid actually thinks their Dad is a nice guy when the punishment is being administered, eh?) Yet, now, we can actually see the love and grace of God even in those extremely painful events.

Today we see this same pattern. Jesus was the new Moses. He came to give a new Law. He didn't write the law of external behaviors on tablets of stone; he wrote the law of internally transforming love on the tablets of people's hearts. It is the law of love and grace. And yet, it is still a law and it is still enforced by the same God who gave the Law to Moses.

One of the most dangerous aspects of grace is that it can be easily taken for granted and manipulated by evil intent. We have been given great freedom, but that freedom was not given for the purpose of self-indulgence. We have been given freedom to be the open conduit of God's love through us, in total surrender to God's will.

When Annanias and Sapphira tried to manipulate the freedom that they experienced in the "New Order," God, the Father of this young society, had to establish God's authority and strike a healthy dose of Holy Fear into the ranks.

Our society that touts "freedom, liberty, and the pursuit of happiness" as the highest of all moral values, shies away from the notion of a God who can illicit fear in the ranks. We immediately think of the images of millions of Muslims bowing in fear before Allah that we have seen on the nightly news. We don't want anything to do with a God who would punish. We want a kinder, gentler God. Let's get one thing straight. Don't mess with God. God is the same yesterday, today, and forever. The same God who opened up the crevice to swallow up the clan of Achan is the same God who poured out the Holy Spirit on the church.

It would do us well to be reminded time and again that God will not be mocked. Let's never be flippant with our worship or with our attitudes toward God. God is the Almighty, Loving, Heavenly Father who loves enough to discipline God's children in order to protect them from themselves.

Just For Kids

Do you like it when your parents punish you when you disobey them? Why?

How do you feel when one of your siblings or a friend is punished when they have disobeyed?

What did Annanias and Sapphira do wrong in the story? How did God feel about it? What happened to them?

Do you think other people in the church were tempted to try the same trick that Annanias and Sapphira did? Why?

God loves us very much, and, just like our parents, sometimes it is necessary for God to punish God's children when they disobey. Spend some time talking about why it is necessary for there to be "justice" in a family and in a society.

For example: What would happen if there were no laws and people were allowed to steal and kill whenever they want? What would life be like?

Remember, it is a good thing to have a little bit of Holy Fear when we think about the Almighty, All-powerful God. It is also good to remember that, although God is almighty, God is our loving Father who would never do anything to harm us, only to correct us and teach us how to love God more deeply.

Acts: The Church is Born
Session 2: Growing Strong in Jerusalem

Lesson 5

Acts 5:12-42

Vv. 12-16 forms the third "portrait" of the first church in Jerusalem. Compare and contrast this passage with Acts 2:42-47 and Acts 4:32-35. What stands out to you about this current description of the church?

What was the result of the presence of this church? (vv. 15-16)

What attitude did the leaders of the religious establishment have towards the church? Why?

How were John and Peter released?

What stance did Peter take in defense of their disobedience (why did they do it)? (vv. 20-32)

Restate Gamaliel's argument in your own words. (vv. 34-39)

For what reason did the apostles rejoice? (v. 41)

Drawn to the Light

We can consider vv. 12-16 as the continuation of the portrait that Luke began to paint of the church in 4:32. It's as if Luke interjected the story of Annanias and Sapphira as a colorful, yet important, side note in the middle of the description.

Here is one simple observation from this portion of the portrait. When the church was courageous enough to be the church, to be filled with God's might presence, even in the face of adversity, then people were drawn to it. They didn't go out and get people ramped up to come to their meetings. They simply WERE the church. When something is real, then people notice. There was power there and people from all over the region began flocking to them to tap into it. Let's remember the simple overflow principle. If we keep first things first, create the space in our hearts for the Holy Spirit to have freedom to transform us, then God will overflow from our authentic self and people will encounter the power of God in us. They will either be drawn to it, or they will hate it. But that is not up to us to decide or to worry about.

Delightful Disgrace

When was the last time you rejoiced over being disgraced? Wouldn't it be amazing if we could get to a place where our highest priority was to be the light of God's power in our world? Wouldn't it be great if the fear of rejection, of looking stupid, of losing our position in society, would not choke out the life-giving flowers of God's Kingdom that long to burst out in a beautiful bouquet in our lives?

Perhaps you could pray a dangerous prayer today. "Lord, please give me the courage to be able to rejoice in suffering disgrace for the sake of your name."

Acts: The Church is Born

Session 2: Growing Strong in Jerusalem

Just For Kids

Tell about a time when you were really embarrassed.

Look up the word disgrace. What does it mean?

Why do you think the apostles were happy about being disgraced in front of everyone in Jerusalem?

In our world there are a lot of people who do not like Jesus. These people even want to hurt or disgrace others who do love and follow Jesus. How would you feel if someone tried to make you look stupid or kept you from having freedom just because you loved and talked openly about Jesus?

While we do not usually experience these things in our country, it is important to remember that right now there are people who are in prison simply because they love Jesus. Take some time to pray for those people, and ask God to help you be sure that you would have a joyful attitude, even if people tried to disgrace you for Jesus' sake.

Acts: The Church is Born

Acts: The Church is Born

Session 3: The Pruning Begins

Introduction

When a tree becomes strong and starts to bear fruit, a good gardener knows that it needs to be pruned. Unless the shears are taken out and the little wild branches cut off, the tree will become unproductive. Cutting off dead wood and trimming up the branches is probably not a pleasant experience for the tree, but in the long run it is the most loving thing that the gardener can do for the tree. The pruning process will allow the tree to become even more fruitful in the future.

The tree of the church has been growing in Jerusalem for a while. It set its roots in week 1. Last week it experienced some good fruit and growth in ministry. This week we see God pull out the trimming shears and allow the church to experience its first real pain.

There was some dead wood of prejudice that was deep set in the hearts of the first believers. God knew that the racial tension in the church would ultimately destroy the mission of reaching the whole world. Through the life of Stephen, God was able to demonstrate what the Kingdom of God and God's Absolute Love was really all about.

This week's reading is all about this young, Grecian Jew, who actually "got it" when it came to the message that Jesus proclaimed. Stephen preached a message that changed the world. Then he gave up his life for his Lord and became the first martyr for Jesus in history. We have much to be thankful for in the life and ministry of Stephen.

Acts: The Church is Born

Session 3: The Pruning Begins

Lesson 1

Acts 6:1-7

What was the controversy in the church?

The Grecian Jews were Jews who were influenced by the Greek culture. Some call them "Hellenistic Jews." They spoke Greek as opposed to the Aramaic language of the "Hebraic Jews." The Grecian Jews were also more open to non-Jewish ideas than the Hebraic Jews. How might these differences have caused problems in the church of Jerusalem?

What was the solution that the "twelve" proposed?

What was the contrast between what the "twelve" were to do be doing and what the "seven" were to be doing?

The word "serve" in v.2 is the infinitive form ("to serve" as opposed to "serving") of the same word that is translated "ministry" in v. 4. In other words this passage could be paraphrased like this, "The seven were called to do the ministry of the table, while the twelve were called to do the ministry of the Word." Does this reading change your understanding of the roles that each group played? If so, how?

How does it make you feel to know that the first church had arguments and controversy? Why?

What are some possible parallels to this problem in the contemporary church? How might they be solved?

Trouble in Paradise

Even the first church didn't get it right. First Annanias and Sapphira. Now cultural tension and prejudice, and the misappropriation of goods. What is going on? After reading the "portraits" of the church in Jerusalem last week, it is easy to believe that they were perfect. It is also easy to become discouraged by the belief that they were perfect and wonder why our church struggles with sin and mistakes. We can take comfort to remember that the people in Jerusalem were human beings, just like you and me, that had deep layers of muck that needed to be flushed out by the Holy Spirit.

While we can take comfort to know that they were not perfect, we should never use this knowledge as a license to become apathetic about sin. God is working with us to bring about change in us. It is a slow process, but it is a continual process. As we study Acts we will see that God gradually takes the church in Jerusalem through a process of transformation. God exposes one layer of muck in their hearts, convicts them of it, delivers them from it, allows them to have victory for a while, and then peels back a new layer. That's how it works. Be comforted to know that the same God who worked with those prejudiced, whining people, is working with you as well.

Roles in the Church

It is important to note two things from the story today regarding roles in the church.

1. The apostles recognized that there were different types of roles within the church and different types of people to perform those functions. Some of the people were called to focus on prayer and the study and teaching of the Word. Others were called to manage and orchestrate the care of the needy. Each person has a role to play, and not all roles are identical.

2. While all roles are not identical, all roles are equally valuable in the eyes of God. Notice the qualifications that were needed for the "servers." This was not some left-over job for the "second-class" members of the church. The administration of care for the widows and orphans was such an important job that the apostles realized that they would continue to botch it up if they did not appoint godly people to do it. These

Acts: The Church is Born

Session 3: The Pruning Begins

"servers" carried the same authority and power that the apostles did (notice that Stephen did great signs and wonders in the city). Just remember, no matter what your role is in the church, it is vital to the health of the body that you see your value and perform your role "as unto the Lord" (Colossians 3:17)

Just For Kids

Have you ever come across someone that was very different than you? What made them different; language, skin color, culture, habits?

How did you feel around that person?

Discuss times in our country's history when people were treated poorly based upon the color of their skin or their ethnic origin. How did this affect our country?

Do you think Jesus wants this kind of thing to happen in the church? Why?

How did the apostles handle it when it happened to the church in our reading today?

Acts: The Church is Born

Session 3: The Pruning Begins

Lesson 2

Acts 6:8-15

How is Stephen described? Compare this description to Acts 2:43 and Acts 7:36. Based upon these parallels, what kind of man can we assume Stephen was?

Use your Atlas and locate the four places from which the members of the "Synagogue of the Freedmen" came – Cyrene, Alexandria, Cilicia, Asia. Considering that the Jews of Jerusalem were prejudiced against any non-Jerusalemite, non-Aramaic speaking Jews, what sort of struggles/issues might these men have had in the city?

What accusations were brought against Stephen? Why?

Compare vv. 12-14 with Mark 14:55-59.

What happened to Stephen's appearance as he was being accused? What could this mean?

Stephen Seized

Two important notes:

1. **Stephen was a Grecian Jew.** It is significant to note that Stephen, a non-Hebraic Jew was described in the same way as the original twelve apostles and as Moses (doing signs and wonders). The story of Stephen is helping the church begin its migration from being simply a sect of Judaism to becoming the global Kingdom of God that Jesus had come to bring.

2. **The city of Tarsus is one of the major cities in the region of Cilicia.** It is very likely that Saul of Tarsus was one of the members of the Synagogue of the Freedmen that killed Stephen. We will see in 8:1 that Luke highlights the fact that Saul was present at Stephen's execution. Then, in chapter 9, this same Saul is thrust into center stage of the story. Just keep this fact in mind as you continue to read the story.

Acts: The Church is Born

Session 3: The Pruning Begins

Just For Kids

How does it make you feel to know that people could gang up on a godly man like Stephen and lie about him in order to get him in trouble? Why?

Why do you think Stephen's face looked like an angel? Draw a picture of this scene where men who hated Stephen were lying about him, but his face looked like an angel.

Remember, even when people do mean things to us, we don't have to behave like they do.

It's time to get your maps out again! Look up and place on your map the four places from which the men in the Synagogue of the Freedmen originated.

Cyrene

Alexandria

Cilicia

Asia

Now find the city of Tarsus. In which of these four regions is the city of Tarsus?

Read Acts 21:39. What important person was from Tarsus? What do you know about this man?

Read Acts 8:1. What part did this man play in Stephen's story?

Acts: The Church is Born

Session 3: The Pruning Begins

Lesson 3

Acts 7:1-19

Where was Abraham when the God of Glory first contacted him?

What relationship did Abraham have with the land that God had promised to him? Did he possess it?

Read Genesis 17:1-14.

Which came first, God's relationship with Abraham or circumcision?

In Romans 4 and Galatians 3, the Apostle Paul teaches the same message that Stephen is trying to communicate to the Sanhedrin. Read Romans 4 and summarize it in your own words. What is the parallel to Stephen's message?

What was the purpose of circumcision?

Where was Joseph when God used him in a mighty way?

What relationship did Joseph have with the "Promised Land" (did he possess it)?

How do you think the High Priest and the religious leaders felt about being lectured by this young man concerning their own history? Why?

Abraham and God

It is interesting to note that of all the great leaders of the early church – Peter, John, Paul – the person who has the longest recorded message is Stephen. Stephen's message in Acts 7 is one of the most important messages ever preached in history. It was the first time that someone, other than Jesus himself, taught the idea that God could be known apart from the Law and apart from the Temple in Jerusalem. Isn't it ironic that it was Stephen, a Grecian Jew, who got it before Peter did?

The point of his message is simply this: God is bigger than any human system – even if God created it. God had an intimate relationship with Abraham before he was circumcised, not because he was circumcised. It was Abraham's faith, not his lack of foreskin that made him right with God. We need to be careful that we never slip into the same trap that the Jews had. They had limited God to a set of rules and a geographical location. The Law and the Temple were just tools to aid in knowing God, not God's self. We will discuss this more tomorrow.

Acts: The Church is Born

Session 3: The Pruning Begins

Just For Kids

Stephen tells the story of Abraham and Joseph. Spend some time retelling the story of these two men as best you can. If you have a children's Bible, you may want to pull that off the shelf and walk through the pictures of this story. (The stories themselves are found in Genesis 12-17 and Genesis 37-45)

How did Joseph's brothers treat him?

How did Joseph treat his brothers? Why?

Read Genesis 50:19-20. What attitude did Joseph have toward the meanness that his brothers showed him?

In what ways is Stephen's story similar to Joseph's?

How will you treat people who are mean to you in the future?

Acts: The Church is Born

Session 3: The Pruning Begins

Lesson 4

Acts 7:20-43

Where and how was Moses raised? Why?

How did Moses understand himself in v. 25?

Realizing that this is pure speculation, how do you think Moses felt when the events of vv. 28-29 took place? Why?

How did God communicate to Moses?

How did God identify Himself?

In v. 35, what irony does Stephen expose concerning Moses' role in God's plan?

What was the mark of God's authority on Moses according to v. 36?

In v.37, what did Moses predict God would do?

How does Stephen describe the words that Moses received on Mt. Sinai?

How did the people respond to Moses' message?

What was the nature of "God's House" from the time of Moses to the time of Solomon?

How does God feel about having a "house?"

What accusation did Stephen make against the leaders of Jerusalem? In what ways is this true?

Acts: The Church is Born

Session 3: The Pruning Begins

A Most Unlikely Candidate

As we discussed yesterday, Stephen's message was presenting the idea to the Jews that God is a living God who is bigger than the Law of Moses and the Temple in Jerusalem. God very rarely operates according to our rules and our expectations. God is the Almighty who can and will do whatever God wants to do, whenever and however God wants to do it.

If God wants to send a boy into slavery in Egypt, God will. If God wants to raise a Hebrew boy in the Pharaoh's palace and then send him into the wilderness for 40 years, God will. If God wants to choose a murderer and a coward to be the leader of God's people, God will. Then God will use the slave boy to deliver God's people. Then God will use the murderer to be the shepherd of God's people.

God is the living God. God is the loving God. God is constantly reaching out to God's people and working with them to bring about transformation in them. If they need a Law to guide them in right living, God will give it. If they need a physical space to be able to catch a glimpse of God's infinite glory, God will allow it. Yet, those temporal and physical things could never become the sum total of the majesty of God. They are just tools.

Stephen figured that out. Stephen was learning that Jesus was not just a rabbi. He wasn't even another man like Moses. He was so much more than that. Jesus was the Supreme Lord of all Heaven and was able to reach all nations with his absolute love.

The prospect of losing control of God is a scary one for those who have all the answers. The Jews were not ready to receive this truth about God. Whenever someone delivers a challenging message, it often is received with hostility. Stephen died to give us this message that opened the door for the world to enter into the presence of God.

Thank you, Lord, that you allowed Stephen to die so that he could present this message of hope to us.

Just For Kids

Today Stephen continues telling his story. He talks about Moses. Just like yesterday, spend some time reviewing the story of Moses. His story is found in Exodus.

Who was Moses?

Where was Moses raised?

What great thing did God use Moses to do for his people?

How did God communicate with Moses? Draw a picture of Moses talking with God at the burning bush.

Did Moses need a temple or a "big house" to be able to know God and talk to him? Why?

How can we talk to God today?

Acts: The Church is Born

Session 3: The Pruning Begins

Lesson 5

Acts 7:44-8:1

What does it mean when someone says, "He is my right hand man"?

Today we are going to focus on the phrase "at the right hand of God" and meditate on the vision that Stephen saw just before he was executed. As you read the following passages, please keep in mind the scene that Stephen was experiencing. He was a godly man. He had done nothing wrong except for helping the needy and boldly proclaiming the truth about Jesus. It is very likely that Stephen was originally a member of the Synagogue of the Freedmen, so he was being railroaded by his own "brothers." He would have had every reason to become bitter and angry toward the injustice he was suffering. Yet, as he courageously spoke the truth of Jesus to his oppressors, he saw a vision of Jesus. Read the following verses and try to imagine what God was communicating to Stephen (and to us) with this image.

> Mark 16:19 – Where did Jesus go after he left his earthly ministry.
>
> Acts 2:32-33 – What authority does Jesus have?
>
> Colossians 3:1-4 – Where should our focus be? Why?
>
> Romans 8:31-39. ***Note:* *Isn't it interesting that Paul is the one that wrote this. This is the same man who witnessed the execution of Stephen.*
>
> What promise do we have since Jesus is at the right hand of the Father?
>
> 1 Peter 3:22 – What authority does Jesus have?
>
> Hebrews 10:11-18 – What resulted from Jesus being seated at the right hand of God?

What attitude did Stephen have about dying?

What attitude did he have toward his killers?

Why?

An Example of Love

The greatest killer in our world is not cancer or AIDS. It is bitterness. Through bitterness the enemy can get hold of our souls and inflict a spiritual cancer that will imprison us in the dark cell of ourselves. This spiritual cancer will bubble up in emotional and physical maladies of all kinds and wreak havoc on our lives and the lives of everyone we contact.

When Jesus came to his people, Israel, they were deeply infected with this spiritual cancer. Israel had been oppressed by many nations over the centuries and had grown bitter and arrogant as a result. One of the greatest aspects of Jesus' ministry was to deliver his people from this dark place of hatred and bitterness. He taught them about it with words like, "Love your enemies and pray for those who persecute you." But, the greatest demonstration of this teaching was when Jesus hung on the cross and uttered the astonishing words, "Father, forgive them."

Jesus demonstrated God's absolute love by giving himself up, into the hands of the Sovereign God, and into the hands of those who hated him and falsely accused him. Instead of retaliating and "getting even" he loved them, to the point of death. Jesus' desire was for his disciples to follow in his footsteps and carry this message of God's absolute love to the world. Unfortunately, as is the case with most transformation stories, this kind of change is a slow process. Jesus' first disciples were Jewish and were raised with these same deep seated, cancerous prejudices. If they were to fulfill Jesus' mission of going to the ends of the Earth, they had to be set free from their bitterness and prejudice.

Acts: The Church is Born

Session 3: The Pruning Begins

The story of Stephen serves as a model to the church (both then and now) of the message that Jesus came to bring to the world. Here Peter, James, and John – all Hebraic Jews – watched as a Grecian Jew was filled with the same power of the Holy Spirit that they had, and wonderfully reflected the love of Jesus as he gave his life for him. As we will find next week, the act of martyrdom ignited the spread of the gospel through an outbreak of persecution on the church. You can be assured that every believer had the image of the angel-faced Stephen at the forefront of their mind whenever they were tempted to become discouraged or embittered because of hard times.

Ask God to search your heart right now and expose to you someone against whom you may be harboring bitterness. Ask God to make real to you the vision of Jesus standing at the right hand of the Father. He is bigger than any wrong that may have been done to you. Let it go, forgive the offender, and let the love and power of God heal you from the inside out.

Just For Kids

Does God live in a house? Why?

Here's the point of Stephen's story. The people that were angry with Stephen believed that God lived in the Temple of Jerusalem and that no one could know God apart from this building. Stephen taught that God was bigger than that and that people from anywhere could know God, through Jesus Christ. The people didn't like his teaching, so they wanted to kill him for it.

Do you think God needs a big church building to live in? Does the church need one to be the church? Why?

Where does God live?

Draw a picture of what Stephen saw just before he was killed?

What does it mean when someone says, "He is my right hand man"?

How does it make you feel to know that God can be found anywhere, anytime and that Jesus is at the right hand of the Father and has all power and authority in the world?

Acts: The Church is Born

Acts: The Church is Born

Session 4: Judea and Samaria

Introduction

The tree continues to grow. Unfortunately, many times it takes adversity and pain to bring about real growth. God used the stoning of Stephen and the subsequent persecution of God's people to drive the disciples out of the comfort zone in Jerusalem and to venture into new territory.

In chapters 8-9, we see the fulfillment of the second part of Jesus' commission in Acts 1:8. This week the message of the Kingdom of God branches out into the regions of Judea and Samaria.

As you can see in the illustration, there are two major paths to the story in these chapters. The first is the process that God used to break down the centuries-old barriers of hostility that existed between the Jews and the Samaritans. In one beautiful moment we will witness the coming together of Hebraic Jews, Grecian Jews, and Samaritans as they bask in the outpouring of the Holy Spirit, bringing the broken pieces of God's family into reconciliation and power.

The second road is that of Saul. The insertion of his story at this point of the narrative serves two purposes. First, with Saul converted, it brought an end to the immediate threat of persecution and allowed the newly expanded church to experience a period of peace. Secondly, it served as a foreshadowing of the upcoming main character of the second half of the story. For now, we meet Saul, and then send him off into obscurity for a season.

Acts: The Church is Born

Session 4: Judea and Samaria

Lesson 1

Acts 8:2-13

What was Saul's mission? Why?

What effect did the persecution have on the believers in Jerusalem? How does this seemingly devastating event play into God's plan and Jesus' instructions?

In order to really understand chapter 8, and to grasp the significant role that this story plays in Luke's theological development, it is important for us to look at who the Samaritans were and what relationship the Samaritans had with the Hebraic Jews.

Read 2 Kings 17.

What happened to the people of Samaria? (Samaria was the capital city of the Northern Kingdom of Israel. In the book of Acts this same area was called Samaria.)

Why did God allow this to happen?

What did the Assyrians do to the captives (v. 24)? How did this affect the region?

How would you describe the people of Samaria?

If you were a Jew, during the book of Acts, who was a descendant of the tribe of Judah, and you worshipped at the Temple in Jerusalem, how do you think you would feel toward the Samaritans?

What affect did Philip's preaching have on the people of Samaria?

What kind of man was Simon? How did the people regard him? Why?

How did Simon view the power that the apostles had? (You'll have to peek into tomorrow's reading and read through v. 25) Why?

In what way was Simon's view of the Holy Spirit skewed? In what ways can you see this concept of God's power being misunderstood in our own culture?

Acts: The Church is Born

Session 4: Judea and Samaria

It's More than Magic

In the 1st century, the practice of the magic arts was widespread across the world. Even though it was officially illegal according to the Roman law, it was common practice among the people. The basis of magic was a belief in the spiritual forces of the universe. Each group had its own names for the spiritual realities. Some thought that they were gods and goddesses, others thought they were the spirits of Earth, Wind, and Fire (not to be confused with the 70s band). The purpose of magic was to use rituals and incantations to harness the powers of the universe in order to accomplish the desires of the magician. In other words, the magician felt that he or she could manipulate the "gods" or the "forces" of the cosmos and bring them into submission to their desires.

Luke places this story in the narrative of Acts for a very specific reason. He wanted to make it crystal clear to his readers that the miracles – the "signs and wonders"—that were associated with the coming of the Holy Spirit were in no way, shape, or form a type of magic. This is important to note because the magicians were able to heal people and perform the same kinds of signs and wonders that the apostles experienced. At the experiential level the phenomenon of the apostles was not uncommon and they could be easily misinterpreted as common magic. Remember the story of Moses' showdown with the magicians of Egypt. To them, Moses' miracles were nothing more than simple parlor tricks.

Luke emphasizes that the work of the Holy Spirit is just that, it is the work of the Holy Spirit, not the magical incantations of the apostles. There are two important points to keep clear when attempting to understand the miracles of Acts and the work of the Holy Spirit. First, the miracles were always associated with the clear teaching of the Word of God and the message of Jesus Christ and his Kingdom. Secondly, the apostles did not conjure up the "magic" to "make things happen." Instead, the apostles were simply humble servants who were willing to go where the Spirit led them and left the activity of the Spirit up to him. Do you see the difference? Magicians sought to control the forces for their own will through manipulation. The follower of Jesus is simply focused on the truth of Jesus' Word and open to be used as a servant, following the will and agenda of God.

Before you dismiss this topic as irrelevant for our lives in the 21st century, be aware that magic is alive and well. In many ways the 21st century and the 1st century are very similar. In both centuries we find ourselves in an extremely diverse, multicultural mixing pot of races, religions, and ideologies. We also find ourselves in a culture where there is no dominant philosophy that governs each person, but rather a general void in the area of real meaning and purpose in the world. People are scrambling to find meaning in a world that is bigger and more confusing than they can handle. In both centuries, given this religious vacuum, people flock to the experiential power that is readily available in the practice of magic.

Here's the deal. There are spiritual forces at play in the universe that are intrinsically intertwined with the physical energy of the universe. In increasing numbers, through what we generically call the "New Age Movement," people are learning that you can, indeed, tap into and harness the "energy" of the universe and use it for your own advantage. This is a reality. The dangerous thing is that the practitioners of this art use incredibly "spiritual" language. They even use Biblical language and speak of being followers of Jesus. There are many people in our world who are performing miracles, in the name of Jesus, but are actually functioning under the basic premise of magic, just like Simon.

So, as followers of Jesus, it is important that we learn the lesson that Luke intended with the story of Simon. A strong temptation that we face when we encounter the power of the Holy Spirit is to desire to harness that power, bottle it up, and sell it as our own. We want to be powerful and do great things. We want God to work through us the way God works through other people. We all want to be Peter who can heal people with his shadow and be the conduit of the Holy Spirit with the touch of our hand. The truth is, however, that we aren't all Peter. Peter was simply a vessel that had been broken down by God and brought into submission to God's will. So, too, should we be careful to not be seduced by the power that is available through the "truly spiritual" who seek to manipulate God to meet their own will. We are humble servants. If God wants to raise someone from the dead through our touch, then we need to be willing to obey that, if God wants us to clean toilets and care for the dying in Calcutta, then we need to be willing to do that, or if God wants us to change our children's diapers and provide a nurturing environment for our family, then we need to be willing to do that as well.

Acts: The Church is Born

Session 4: Judea and Samaria

Just for Kids

In our story today, we meet a man who practices magic. When you hear the word "magic" what comes to your mind?

What kind of things was this man able to do?

How did the people react to what he did? Why?

It is important to understand that there are two kinds of magic. The first is an entertainment that is called illusion. This kind of "magic" is simply the art of learning how to trick people's eyes with illusions, like pulling a quarter from behind your ear or making a handkerchief disappear in your hand. These are simply tricks that can be learned. They are fun and harmless.

There is another kind of magic, however, that is not fun and harmless. Simon practiced this kind of magic. It is called witchcraft, sorcery, divination, fortune telling, etc. The reason it is important to bring this up in the study today is because you will be exposed to this kind of magic on television, movies, and other forms of media everyday. In our world, people think that making potions, casting spells, and reading fortunes is fun and harmless. Some even say that it is good for you and is what God wants. As a follower of Jesus it is important to understand that magic of this kind is not from God at all. There are spiritual forces in the universe that are powerful and dangerous. Because God is our loving Father, God does not want us to get hurt by them.

Read Deuteronomy 18:9-13 and Galatians 5:19-21 to find out how God feels about magic.

Spend some time talking with your parents about any ways that you may have been exposed to this kind of magic – either on TV or at school. It is important to tell your parents about these kinds of things so that your heart will stay clean and you will be safe.

Acts: The Church is Born

Session 4: Judea and Samaria

Lesson 2

Acts 8:14-25

Why did Peter and John go to Samaria?

Why would this event have required a special investigation by Peter and John?

What special event happened when Peter and John placed their hands on the Samaritan believers?

What questions does this raise for you? Why?

Review Acts 6:1-6. What was the ethnic tension present in the church of Jerusalem? What kind of Jew was Peter? What kind of Jew was Philip? What kind of ethnic tension existed between the Jews and the Samaritans?

Observation: In this story we see a Grecian Jew presenting the message, a Hebraic Jew (and a founding apostle) endorsing the event, and a group of Samaritans receiving the promised Holy Spirit at the hands of a Jew. This is truly a miracle and the first glimpse of the kind of Kingdom that Jesus intended to bring to the Earth.

Breaking Down the Wall

Look at the title of the study this week: Judea and Samaria. In our culture, that would be like saying "Nazi and Jew" or "KKK and African American" or "Israeli and Palestinian." The Jews and the Samaritans hated each other. The point of this lesson is to understand that the Kingdom of God, the "Good News" that Jesus brought, was that, in God's eyes, there is no distinction between ethnicity.

When God made the covenant to Abraham, God promised that through Abraham's nation all nations would be blessed. Unfortunately, Abraham's descendents forgot about that. Instead they turned to idolatry which led to inner corruption which led to a civil war that ripped the nation apart. Since the day Jeroboam stormed out of Jerusalem and said, "I don't need you people, I can do things the way I want, and to blazes with this stinking family!" things never worked well for the nation. The family was torn in two between the northern Kingdom of Israel and the Southern Kingdom of Judah. Israel was steeped in witchcraft and was eventually destroyed by the Assyrians. Judah wrestled through cycles of idolatry and obedience, until it was finally destroyed by the Babylonians. 500 years later, the beautiful child of God, called Israel, lay in a miserable heap of wounded brothers who hate each other and harbor deep roots of bitterness and resentment as they squabble over theological issues.

The Hebraic Jews neglected the Grecian Jews and the Grecian Jews looked down on the Hebraic Jews. We saw that last week. Both the Hebraic Jews and the Grecian Jews despised the Samaritans. How could God possibly bless the world through the conduit of Israel when it was so deeply divided as a nation?

It is against this backdrop that Acts 8 is told. One of the biggest questions raised in this chapter is "Why did the Holy Spirit not pour out on the Samaritans when they believed?" The best way to make sense of this question is to see it against this cultural and political backdrop. Philip was a Grecian Jew. We saw in ch. 6 that the Grecian Jews were struggling with issues in the church between them and the Hebraic Jews. Had the Holy Spirit come upon the Samaritans at the hands of Philip it would have opened up the church to the possibility of creating factions between the three entities. Some Hebraic Jews could have invalidated the experience as being some kind of magical masquerade that was done at the hands of "those meddling Greeks and Samaritans." God, in his sovereign grace and love for God's family, allowed the Holy Spirit to

Acts: The Church is Born

Session 4: Judea and Samaria

be kept at bay in order to force Peter and John to go and investigate.

"Believing Samaritans," they must have thought to themselves, "this is impossible. We need to check it out for ourselves."

So then, we see a beautiful snapshot of the Kingdom of God. In this scene, we have a Hebraic Jew, a Grecian Jew, and a Samaritan all standing together. Only then did God allow the Spirit to pour out and draw these warring factions into a bond of peace. Once again Abraham's family is healed and brought into unity so that God can fulfill God's promise and bless the world through them.

Here's the irony of this passage. This beautiful picture of unity in the body of Christ that comes through humble submission to the movement of the Holy Spirit and openness to God's love for all people has become one of the greatest stumbling blocks and tools for dissension in the church over the past century. Some people have said that this story proves that there is a concept called the second baptism of the Holy Spirit that comes only through the laying on of hands from God's anointed and that this process is the only way it can legitimately happen. Others in the church disagree and say that the stories of Acts were only true for that generation and there are no supernatural manifestations in the modern church. The church has become polarized, divided, and vindictive toward one another much the same way the Kingdom of Israel and the Kingdom of Judah were in the Old Testament.

As we study through Acts we will learn one important truth. When the Holy Spirit shows up he never has a pattern. Sometimes he fills people before baptism, sometimes he comes after baptism. Sometimes there is the presence of speaking in tongues, sometimes there isn't. Sometimes there is no mention of any signs involved. In Acts 8, the Spirit was kept back in order to bring unity in the body. The point is that it was God's choice, not the disciples. If there is one thing that we can learn from Acts it's that we do not get to dictate to God how, when, or where God can work or what it will look like when God does. He is God and we are not. We are simply called to be submitted to God and open to be obedient to God's directions.

In John 17 Jesus prayed that his people would be one, just as he and the Father are one. May we, as a church, allow ourselves to be open to the mysterious ways of God and realize that we can't tell God what to do or how to do it. Our job is to love one another and simply obey the leading of the Holy Spirit.

Just for Kids

What does the phrase "they fight like cats and dogs" mean?

Who are some groups of people that you know of in our world that "fight like cats and dogs?" Why do they have such a hard time getting along?

In the world during the writing of Acts, the Jews and Samaritans were like cats and dogs. They hated each other and had been like that for hundreds of years. Knowing that these two groups of people hated each other makes our story even more incredible. Here we see Jews and Samaritans coming together and becoming united through the Spirit of God.

That is what the Kingdom of God is all about – bringing people together to break down their hatred for each other and share in God's love together.

Are there any people in your life that you have a hard time loving? Why? Spend some time praying for them today. Ask God to let God's Spirit give you the power to love that person.

Acts: The Church is Born

Session 4: Judea and Samaria

Lesson 3

Acts 8:26-40

It's time to use your Bible Atlas again. Where is Gaza? Is it north or south from Jerusalem?

What can you observe about the position, character and religious beliefs of the eunuch?

Where is Ethiopia? What kinds of people live there? (This is not found in the text, but the same kind of people live there today)

Through what line of reasoning and explanation did Philip explain the message of Jesus? Why?

What role does the Holy Spirit play in this story? How does the role of the Holy Spirit differ in this story from the story of the Samaritans? Why do you suppose the difference exists?

Where does Philip end up? (Keep this in mind for next week)

God of the Globe

Throughout history the term "Christianity" came to be identified as a European institution. In the Middle Ages this was so true that the Geographical region of Western Europe was called "Christendom."

In our reading today we have a refreshing reminder that from the very beginning the message of Jesus was spread to all parts of the world. Yesterday we saw that Philip went to the north and brought the message to the Samaritans. Today he went to the south and brought the message to the Ethiopians.

We must keep this in context. To the Roman mind, Ethiopia was on the farthest southern edge of the world. They really could not conceive of anything beyond it since the majority of the northern region of Africa was spanned by the impassable Sahara desert. Ethiopia was the southernmost region of the Red Sea, beyond which lay only mystery for the Roman mind.

For our cultural context it is important to note one simple thing: the Ethiopians are very dark skinned. Here this – Christianity is not white man's religion! In this story we see the gospel reaching Africa in the infancy of the church. From church history we discover that some of the original apostles journeyed far east and took the message of Jesus to India and Asia. God's design from the very beginning was that all people would know God's love and be in unity with one another. Over time, due to various political issues, the early church became divided and the Asian and African church was cut off from the European church. It is one of the greatest tools of Satan to divide the church across ethnic and doctrinal lines in order to keep us focused on our differences so that we cannot acknowledge the love of God.

In our world of global communication and a growing interchange between cultures, we have an opportunity that was never before possible. We can begin to build bridges of unity between the Western Church, the African church, and the Asian church. We are one body, with one Spirit, and one Lord. Imagine what could happen if there was true, global unity in the body of Christ.

If nothing else, may this study be a simple awareness tool to always remember that whatever ethnic origin you may be from, it is not the center of the universe. We are all parts in God's family. May we ride off today, like the Ethiopian eunuch, rejoicing in the kaleidoscopic Kingdom of God!

Acts: The Church is Born

Session 4: Judea and Samaria

Just for Kids

Today we are going to look at our maps again.

Find Samaria and mark it on your map.

Now find Ethiopia. (You may have to look at a world map)

Today we need to look at a fact that many people tend to forget. The message of Jesus has been in Africa since the beginning. The Ethiopian Eunuch took the message back with him and the church began. Today the Christian church in Ethiopia is the oldest church in the world. Because the story of Acts focuses just on the events that happen around the Mediterranean Sea in southern Europe, it is easy to forget that other apostles took the message to Asia and Africa. God loves the whole world, not just a certain kind of person from a certain place.

There is a lot of famine, war, and disease in Ethiopia right now and they need prayer and assistance. Spend some time praying for the people in Ethiopia and ask God to heal the people there.

Acts: The Church is Born

Session 4: Judea and Samaria

Lesson 4

Acts 9:1-30

What does the tern "meanwhile" mean in the flow of a story?

When we last saw Saul (ch. 7) what was he doing?

What was Saul's intention for going to Damascus? Why?

Who appeared to Saul on the way to Damascus? How?

What physical affects did this encounter have on Saul?

What spiritual affects did this encounter have on Saul?

If you were Ananias, and had heard that Saul was coming to persecute your church, what struggles may have you had at the Lord's request?

How did Jesus describe Saul in vv. 15-16? What would his life be like from this point on?

What role does the Holy Spirit play in Saul's conversion? How is this account similar or different from previous stories in Acts (Acts 2 at Pentecost; Acts 8 with the Samaritans; Acts 8 with the Eunuch) regarding the role and activity of the Holy Spirit?

In what ways is the choosing of Saul a great irony? Why?

How did the people of Damascus respond to the new Saul? Why?

Who came to Saul's defense and aid in Jerusalem?

Why did Saul get shipped off to Tarsus?

Acts: The Church is Born

Session 4: Judea and Samaria

An Unlikely Candidate

Here are two simple observations from this very famous story:

1. God seems to use the most unlikely candidates to do God's work. On the morning that Saul left for Damascus no one would have ever predicted that this man would become a great ambassador for the message that he was trying to stamp out. Saul was a man that was highly educated and incredibly zealous for the politics of Jerusalem. Having been born in Tarsus, a city on the southern coast of Turkey, Saul was both a Roman citizen and a Greek by culture. However, by choice he submitted himself to the rabbinical training of the Pharisees in Jerusalem and was fast moving up the ladder of power. No doubt this rampage to Damascus would bode well for his future in the Sanhedrin Council. Indeed, this man was a ball of energetic, but misguided potential. So Jesus stopped him in his tracks and changed his life forever.

2. God put Saul on the backburner of obscurity for 13 years before he resurfaced. Throughout scripture we see the repeated story that God leads God's future leaders through an experiential desert before he allows them to emerge as broken and purified vessels for God. Saul is not exception. On the day that he sailed for Tarsus there were probably many heads swagging in the Sanhedrin council, mourning the loss of such great potential. "What a waste, such a good mind, blinded and left on the scrap heap," they may have thought. And then he was gone from the radar. That must have been difficult for Saul to accept. Yet, it was through that time that God prepared him for the journeys that lay ahead.

Here is a challenge for today. When you meet someone in the course of your life, don't be too quick to pass judgment on them. Had you met Saul on the day of Stephen's stoning you would have most likely dismissed him as a lost cause. Also, if you meet someone who seems to be a nobody, don't be too quick to treat them as such. Had you met Saul on his boat ride to Tarsus, you may have not even noticed him and looked for someone really important with which to associate.

These same lenses can be used for your view of yourself. If you are experiencing a dry time in your life, or if you feel like you don't deserve the difficult circumstances in your life, just remember that God could very well be preparing you for something of which you cannot even currently imagine. Remember, its God's Kingdom and God's timing, not ours.

Acts: The Church is Born

Session 4: Judea and Samaria

Just for Kids

Today it would be fun to act out the story of Saul on the road to Damascus. You will need three main players. If you have more than three, the remaining players can be Saul's companions on the road.

Players:

Saul – he is angry with the followers of Jesus and wants to go to Damascus to round them up and throw them in jail.

Jesus – we only hear his voice as he flashes a bright light at Saul and stops him in his tracks.

Ananias – he is a follower of Jesus that is scared of Saul. Jesus asks him to be kind to Saul and help him discover how to become of follower of Jesus.

The scene

Have Saul and his companions start on one end of the room. We'll call this Jerusalem. Ananias sits at the other end of the room. This is Damascus. Jesus stands in the middle of the room, either under a light or holding a flashlight.

Action

Saul acts angry and says,

> "I'm going to get those Jesus followers and I've got the papers to put them in the slammer!"
> (Have some paper rolled up like a scroll)

He storms across the room toward Damascus.

Jesus:
> "Saul, Saul, why do you persecute me?"

Saul: "Who are you?"

Jesus: "I am Jesus, whom you are persecuting," he replied. "Now get up and go into the city, and you will be told what you must do."

Place a bandana or blindfold around Saul's eyes. His companions lead him to Damascus.

Ananias is sitting in a position of prayer.

Jesus:
> Ananias!

Ananias:
> Yes, Lord?

Jesus:
> Go to the house of Judas on Straight Street and ask for a man from Tarsus named Saul, for he is praying. In a vision he has seen a man named Ananias come and place his hands on him to restore his sight

Ananias:
> "I have heard many reports about this man and all the harm he has done to your saints in Jerusalem. And he has come here with authority from the chief priests to arrest all who call on your name

Jesus:
> Go! This man is my chosen instrument to carry my name before the Gentiles and their kings and before the people of Israel. I will show him how much he must suffer for my name

Ananias puts his hand on Saul.

Ananias
> Brother Saul, the Lord—Jesus, who appeared to you on the road as you were coming here—has sent me so that you may see again and be filled with the Holy Spirit."

Take the blindfold off of Saul. Saul praises God and Ananias baptizes him.

End of play

How do you think Ananias felt when Jesus said that Saul was coming?

How do you think Saul felt when he was blind? How did he feel when his sight was restored?

Isn't it amazing that God likes to choose the least likely candidate to be God's tool?

Acts: The Church is Born

Session 4: Judea and Samaria

Lesson 5

Acts 9:31-43

Let's look closely at v. 31.

What are the three geographical regions mentioned to describe the church? How is this different from the first portrait of the church painted in Acts 2:42-47?

What did God, through the Holy Spirit, do for the church?

In what attitude did the church operate?

OK, get out your maps again. Where are Lydda and Joppa?

What miracle was performed in Lydda? To whom was credit given for this miracle?

What effect did the miracle have on the people of the area?

What kind of a person was Dorcas?

What miracle happened concerning Dorcas?

How did this miracle affect that city?

A Time of Peace

This little passage in the story of Acts is a transitional passage that serves two important purposes.

First, it demonstrates a picture of the Kingdom of God in its original design. When the peace of God rules, then there is healing and resurrection. The Kingdom of God, ruled by the Prince of Peace, floods its people with life, purpose, and energy. We, as citizens of this Kingdom, can be focused and able to live in the full health of God's loving design for humanity. While this is the standard and the ideal, we must remember that we live in the reality of being "already, but not yet." This snapshot of the Kingdom is the ideal. It provides a picture of the hope that keeps us going. Yet, the reality is that we still live in a world that is inundated with forces that are contrary to God's peace. We are still at war. Peter, the one who was a conduit of healing and resurrection was, himself, crucified at the hands of an evil empire. In this passage the Holy Spirit, through the hands of the author Luke, gives us that refreshing reminder that things can be different. There can be peace. We just need to keep our eyes focused on Jesus.

The second purpose for the passage is to set us up for the next part of the story. Peter has just come through what must have seemed to him as a huge struggle and breakthrough in his spiritual transformation. God had just stretched him beyond his imagination when God used him to bring the Holy Spirit to the Samaritans. But now, after the uncomfortable stretching process was over, we see Peter freely passing through an ethnically mixed region and experiencing a substantial level of peace and a moment of basking in the peaceful bliss of the realized Kingdom of God. He had just come out of a difficult valley and was twirling on the mountain top.

Here's the thing about the spiritual journey of transformation. Enjoy the mountain top while you have it, because it is often just the quiet before another storm of God's stretching process in your life. Peter was about to experience a stretch that he had never imagined. In chapter 9 he may have felt that he had reached the goal. After all, God had reconciled the nation of Israel through bond of peace. Israel was whole; God's covenant promise to Abraham was being fulfilled. From now on it would be smooth sailing. When he got to Joppa he thought he would just take a little breather on Simon the Tanner's roof and meditate in the blissful peace of God's kingdom. Little did he know that a

Acts: The Church is Born

Session 4: Judea and Samaria

message from God was coming that would blow him away! But that's for next week.

For now, let's always keep the hope of God's ideal in mind. And remember that even through the valleys when God stretches us, we can know this same peace. As the apostle Paul wrote in Colossians 3:12 "Let the peace of Christ rule in your hearts, since as members of one body you were called to peace."

Just for Kids

Do you know what the word "Shalom" means? It is the Hebrew word for peace. In the Hebrew, to wish someone "Shalom" meant that you hoped their whole life was healthy and safe.

When Peter healed Aeneas and raised Dorcas from the dead he was demonstrating what real "Shalom" looks like. In the Kingdom of God there is real peace and real health.

In this world we still struggle with sickness and death. How does it make you feel when you know that people get sick and die every day?

How would you feel if everyone could be healed from their sickness and not have to die?

Jesus said that his Kingdom would be like that. Sometimes God allows us to witness miracles of healing and resurrection in this life, and that is awesome. We should pray for that. Yet, the real hope of "Shalom" is that someday we will experience Jesus' Kingdom in its complete state. In that day there will be no sickness and no death.

How does it make you feel to know that you can have God's "Shalom" today?

Acts: The Church is Born

Acts: The Church is Born

Session 5: Crossing the Great Divide

Introduction

Throughout history there have been events that have marked the beginning of a new era; the invention of the printing press, the first telegraph message, the first man on the moon. After these events, the world was never the same and people's minds were opened to whole new vistas of possibilities. In our reading this week we come across just such an event.

Up to this point in the story the good news of Jesus has been spread to Judea and Samaria, within the confines of the covenant God made with Abraham. (A case could be made that the Ethiopian was actually a Jewish convert). In other words, the Kingdom of God was simply being restored to its original design. We saw how much this stretched Peter last week and how God had allowed him a respite of peace. This week Peter is about to face his greatest challenge. He is about to step across the great chasm of racism and learn that God loves Gentiles and desires for all people to be included in God's Kingdom.

In the second half of the week we see the beginning of great changes in the church. In preparation for the launch of the "ends of the earth" campaign, we begin to see a shifting of focus away from Jerusalem as the center of the church and notice that God has a special place for the multicultural melting pot called Antioch. As Herod, the false king of the Jews, falls under his own pride, the true King of the Jews, Jesus, is positioning his forces to conquer the world with grace, peace, and most of all love for all people.

Acts: The Church is Born

Session 5: Crossing the Great Divide

Lesson 1

Acts 10:1-48

Read the following description of Caesarea.

> Named in honour of the Roman emperor Caesar Augustus, it was the Roman metropolis of Judaea and the official residence both of the Herodian kings and the Roman procurators....
>
> The city was lavishly adorned with palaces, public buildings and an enormous amphitheatre, dominated by Herod's huge temple dedicated to Caesar and Rome.... Like other NT Mediterranean communities, Caesarea had a mixed population, making for inevitable clashes between Jews and Gentiles.[1]

Based upon this description, how do you think the devout Jews felt about Caesarea? Why?

What qualities/behaviors did Cornelius demonstrate that "got God's attention?"

How is this portrait of Cornelius different from the image the Jews must have had when they envisioned a Roman centurion?

Read Leviticus 11. This was the Law that Peter had been taught from the time he was a child. How do you think he felt when he saw the vision of the animals in the sheet and was told to eat?

Read Mark 7:18-19. What did Jesus teach about food?

According to v.28, why is this scene so radical?

What was Cornelius' attitude in v.33? Why is it important to have this attitude?

What realization did Peter finally come to regarding the nature of God? Why was this such an important paradigm shift, not only for Peter, but for the church as a whole?

Here we have another account of the Holy Spirit being poured out on a group of people (similar to Pentecost and the Samaritans). Observe the sequence of events that surrounded this occurrence: baptism, belief, laying on of hands, tongues, etc. How does this compare to the other accounts?

Acts: The Church is Born

Session 5: Crossing the Great Divide

Crossing the Great Divide

Peter's vision on the tanner's roof must have been one of the most confusing moments of his life. Try to place yourself in his shoes (or sandals). For his entire life he had been taught that it was wrong to eat certain types of food. In fact, it wasn't just wrong, it was a sin and doing so would cause God to reject you as an unclean person. Compounded with this teaching was the notion that the reason the world was so bad was because so many people were not obeying these rules and these "unclean" people were polluting our society and they must be avoided at all costs. Even associating with them would spoil you, corrupt you, and bring the wrath of God down on your head.

Now, look into the sheet that is full of unclean animals and hear the voice that says, "Take and eat." What?!? Surely not, Lord. That is you, right God? I mean, how could you possibly ask me to do this?

At this point we (as the reader) must stop and make a very important decision. Is this the voice of God, or is this an imposter that was impersonating the voice of God and asking Peter to do something that would disobey God and bring God's wrath down on his head and throw the church into a wrong turn that would destroy it forever? The answer to this question will determine how you interpret the rest of Scripture.

If

a) this is an imposter, then we might as well throw the rest of the Bible out and forget about it, because the rest of the New Testament hinges upon this story.

b) this was truly God's voice, then we need to come to grips with the fact that God asked Peter to do something that appeared to be a sin in Peter's mind.

Here are some thoughts and observations:

1. **Perhaps it wasn't that God was contradicting God's self, perhaps it was that Peter's theology, as it had been handed down to him through generations of teachers, had become fundamentally distorted and had strayed from the core of God's heart and intention.** When God gave the dietary laws to the slaves in Egypt, God was protecting them from disease and pestilence in an environment that was very hostile to their survival. They were untrained as a nation and they were moving into cultures that undoubtedly carried disease that was foreign to their systems. Because God is a loving God who cares about God's people, and because God's intent for Abraham's family was to be a blessing to all nations, God instituted dietary laws. Throughout the centuries these laws had become distorted and had evolved into a tool to drive a wedge between nations. By Peter's day the dietary laws had become a badge of honor that set the Jewish people apart from the "heathen." They also became a litmus test of holiness that would keep the wrath of God at bay and prove one's worth in the kingdom. The law that had given life in its conception now bred death and destruction. God was not contradicting God's self; he was confronting distortion and beginning the liberation process for Peter and the church.

2. **Following God is a scary and unpredictable endeavor.** Look at the great stories of the leaders in the Bible – Abraham, Joseph, Moses, David, Elijah. When was God tame and predictable in those stories? God told Abraham to go into the unknown, with no map or instruction book; only a relationship with God. God threw Joseph into a dungeon with no explanation or hope. He only had faith. God led Moses with a wild pillar of fire and smoke, and led him on unpredictable paths through the wilderness. God allowed David to enter the holy place and he didn't die. David followed God with his heart as he bumbled around with his own sinfulness. Elijah knew God well enough to call for rain and hear God's gentle whisper in the cleft of the rock. Each of these men did not follow a predictable, law-bound God. Instead, they were in relationship with the infinite, Almighty, and they obeyed God as God led.

Today, Peter begins that journey with God. Get up and eat. Now go and extend the right hand of fellowship to the man who represents all that you have been told is evil in the world. Step across the great divide and allow God to do God's work in spite of your shortsightedness.

Acts: The Church is Born

Session 5: Crossing the Great Divide

Here is the message for the church today. Many times we become focused on the "laws" that we have created. "Good Christians" do this and "Good Christians" DON'T do that! "Oh, I can't believe he went and did _____! I thought he was a Christian? We must no longer associate with them."

Remember, in the Sermon on the Mount, Jesus brought us a new law. He called us to holiness; to perfection. Yet, the perfection he called us to was not about what we do or don't do on the outside. He called us to grow in the perfection of God's unconditional, absolute love. We are called to love the unlovely, the sick, the enemy, and the "unclean."

Where are the dividing walls today? Are there any places in our hearts where we find the self-righteous tendencies that so easily creep up and place us in the camp with the Pharisees? Are there any people, Christian or not, that we consider to be "unclean" because of the things that they do on the outside of their body, before we ever take the time to examine the inside of their heart? Perhaps we can walk across the bridge of God's Kingdom alongside of Peter and reach out a hand today.

Just For Kids

Have some fun acting out the story of Peter's vision. Get a blanket or a sheet and fill it with your stuffed animals. Have one person pretend to be Peter while he was taking a nap. Have a couple people hold the sheet in front of Peter.

God said, "Take and eat!"

Peter replied, "Surely not, Lord! I have never eaten anything impure or unclean."

God said, ""Do not call anything impure that God has made clean."

This happened three times.

Why was Peter not willing to eat the animals that he saw in the sheet? (Read Leviticus 11 for a clue)

Have you ever had a time when your parents asked you to do something that was against one of the rules that they had made? Think of a time when this would be appropriate.

Here are two things to keep in mind:
1. God is the one who makes up the rules, when he says it's OK to do something, then it is OK.
2. We don't get to break God's rules just because we think it's OK. God is the only one who gets to make that decision.

In both cases we need to remember that God is in charge, not us.

Acts: The Church is Born

Session 5: Crossing the Great Divide

Lesson 2

Acts 11:1-18

How was Peter received when he arrived in Jerusalem? Why?

What association did Peter make between the encounter with Cornelius and the teaching of Jesus? How did this event impact Peter's theology?

How did it affect the theology of the church in Jerusalem?

In what ways do you see the church in our contemporary culture getting stuck on some theological distortions in the same way the Jewish Christians like Peter had become?

In what ways could God be trying to break us free from these distorted views?

Read and meditate on:

Romans 10:12

Galatians 3:28

Colossians 3:11

Peter's Transformation

Today we are reminded of a very important Bible study principle. Whenever something is repeated in Scripture, it is a strong indication that this is a very important thing that needs to be given attention. In today's reading we see the duplication of Peter's experience with Cornelius. Luke could have easily said that Peter simply told them what happened and saved himself a lot of precious parchment space. The fact that he launches into a second recounting of the story tells us that Luke saw this story as crucial to the overall message of Acts.

Here are three thoughts for today:

This story is crucial for the message of Acts. We discussed this yesterday. The Kingdom of God is about fulfilling God's promise to Abraham that God would bless all nations. Racism and prejudice of any kind is one of the greatest hindrances to the love of God that exists in our world.

When you obey God's wild call, you will often be misunderstood by fellow Christians. The majority of Jesus followers love to have safety nests and rules to follow. When there are clear-cut rules and life is black-and-white, then things are much easier to manage. That's fine. Many people function best this way and God can definitely bless that and use it. However, God also calls God's people to push the envelope and shake things up from time to time. If God is calling you to do that, just remember Peter. The believers back at Jerusalem gave him a lot of heat for what he did with Cornelius. People are resistant to change and God's change-agents tend to be unpopular people much of the time.

Change is hard, even for the change-agent. It is comforting to realize that Peter was in process himself. He did not fully understand what was happening around him or the role that God had used him in to turn the religious scene on its ear. Peter was simply obedient. Later on in the story we'll see that Peter continued to struggle with the racial tension that was deep inside his own soul. However, the lesson we need to follow is found in Peter's simple statement, "Who was I to think that I could oppose God?" May this be our attitude each day. We are called not necessarily to understand, but simply to obey when God says, "Go!"

Acts: The Church is Born

Session 5: Crossing the Great Divide

Just For Kids

Read the following verses

>   Romans 10:12
>   Galatians 3:28
>   Colossians 3:11

What do these verses tell us about how God feels about the difference between boys and girls, nationalities, and cultures?

What are some cultures that you don't understand or seem so different to you that you might be a little bit afraid of it? Spend some time praying for that culture and asking God to show you how you could learn to love that culture the way God does.

Acts: The Church is Born

Session 5: Crossing the Great Divide

Lesson 3

Acts 11:19-30

Read the following article that describes the city of Antioch.

> Antioch on the Orontes, now Antakya in SE Turkey, some 500 km N of Jerusalem, was founded c. 300 BC by Seleucus I Nicator after his victory over Antigonus at Issus (310 BC). It was the most famous of sixteen Antiochs established by Seleucus in honour of his father. Built at the foot of Mt Silpius, it overlooked the navigable river Orontes and boasted a fine seaport, Seleucia Pieria. While the populace of Antioch was always mixed, Josephus records that the Seleucids encouraged Jews to emigrate there in large numbers, and gave them full citizenship rights (Ant. 12.119).
>
> Antioch fell to Pompey in 64 BC, and he made it a free city. It became the capital of the Roman province of Syria, and was the third largest city of the empire. The Seleucids and Romans erected magnificent temples and other buildings.
>
> Even under the Seleucids the inhabitants had gained a reputation for energy, insolence and instability, which manifested itself in a series of revolts against Roman rule. Nevertheless, Antioch was renowned for its culture, being commended in this respect by no less a person than Cicero (Pro Archia 4). Close by the city were the renowned groves of Daphne, and a sanctuary dedicated to Apollo, where orgiastic rites were celebrated in the name of religion. Despite the bad moral tone, life in Antioch at the beginning of the Christian era was rich and varied.[2]

What was unique about the ministry of those from Cypress and Cyrene as opposed to those from Jerusalem?

Why did the church in Jerusalem send Barnabas to Antioch?

Read the following description of Tarsus.

> The coinage of the period suggests a mingling of Greek and Oriental influence....The Tarsus of Paul, [was a] synthesis of East and West, Greek and Oriental.[3]

Given the fact that Saul was born in Tarsus, and had been there for several years since his conversion, why do you suppose Barnabas went to get him?

What was the nature of Barnabas and Saul's ministry in Antioch?

What was the role of the prophet in the church in Antioch?

How did the church in Antioch respond to the prophet's message? What does this tell you about the character of this church?

Acts: The Church is Born

Session 5: Crossing the Great Divide

A Shift in Center

Society longs to have a center. It needs to have a place from which and to which all ideas flow. For the Roman Empire it was the city of Rome that lay at the center of its people. For centuries it was Jerusalem that lay at the center of the Jewish culture. At the center of Jerusalem was the Temple with all of its pomp and circumstance. In that house it was believed that the presence of God made God's dwelling.

In our story today, Luke drives home one of the major themes of Acts. Luke continually teaches us that there is no political or geographical center to the Kingdom of God. To demonstrate this point we see that the center of influence in the early church began to drift from Jerusalem to the city of Antioch.

This shift makes sense for two reasons:

1. **Theologically**. God was communicating to God's people that it was not the physical Temple and the racially exclusivistic Jews that comprised the Kingdom; rather it was the cosmopolitan kaleidoscope of humanity that comprised the Kingdom of God. Being the third largest city in the Empire and a melting pot of races, Antioch was the perfect choices to give a physical representation of what the Kingdom was supposed to look like.

2. **Practically**. There was a practical reason to choose this city as well. The Kingdom was about to launch on its "ends of the Earth" campaign. In order for this to happen it needed a centralized sea port. Jerusalem was land-locked and not conducive to world-travel. Antioch, on the other hand, was situated on the Orontes River and had a port a Seleucia at the mouth of the river where it emptied into the Mediterranean sea. We'll discover that this multicultural city became God's launching pad for the Kingdom's expansion into the Roman Empire.

Just For Kids

Let's get those maps out again. Our passage today mentions four places. Find them and place them on your map:

Phoenicia

Cyprus

Antioch

Cyrene

When the believers from Jerusalem went to Antioch, did they preach the Gospel to everyone? Why or why not?

To whom did the believers from Cyprus and Cyrene preach the good news of Jesus? Why do you think they did that?

One important lesson that we are learning from Acts is that it is wrong to leave people out simply because they are different. God loves all people and wants everyone to know about Jesus. It is important for us to make sure that we never ignore someone or think badly about someone simply because they come from another country or have a different skin color than our own.

Acts: The Church is Born

Session 5: Crossing the Great Divide

Lesson 4

Acts 12:1-17

Herod -- There were many Herods in history. The Herod we meet in this text is the grandson of "Herod the Great" – the one who killed all the boys under the age of 2 in the story of Jesus' birth. The Herod in this text is not, however, the same Herod (Herod Antipas) that had John the Baptist executed in the Gospels. By the time of Acts ch.12, Herod the King, also known as Agrippa (Father of the Agrippa found later in Acts), had been given authority by the Roman government to rule over Galilee, Perea, Judea, and Samaria.

Why do you suppose God allowed James to be killed and while He spared Peter through a miraculous prison escape?

How well was Peter guarded? Why do you suppose such precautions were taken to guard him this way?

What was Peter's initial misperception of the angelic visit?

How did the disciples respond to the news that Peter was at the door? Why?

If James was killed in v. 2, who is the James that Peter refers to in v. 17?

Of Pain and Prayer

Sometimes good people die. One of the greatest unanswered questions in the scripture has to do with the death of James. Why did he die when Peter was spared? Why was his death glossed over when Stephen's got so much ink? Wasn't James one of the three disciples that formed Jesus' inner circle? How could he just die so suddenly with no fanfare?

Here's the answer…we don't know. We have to believe that people were praying for him, and yet his life was not spared. Were they not praying hard enough? Was he living in sin? There is no indication to say that these things were true. So, why did it happen?

A missionary once said, "I am immortal until God is done with me." That's really the bottom line. If we understand that life isn't about us – we aren't the hero of the story – and that we are simply playing our part in the grand story, then we will be OK with the fact that some people will get to live out the miracle stories while other people will live, and die, in relative obscurity. In God's Kingdom there is no such thing as the insignificant or the obscure, because God sees it all and cares for it all. God cares about the anthill that was washed away by the rain as much as God cares about the coastline that was washed away by the Tsunami. It is all important to God.

Just this week I received word that two missionaries in Guyana were murdered in their home. They were Wycliffe translators who had been working for years to bring the Word of God in to a tribal language. They were close to completion, but they were killed. Why? We don't know. We don't know why some Christians are miraculously healed of cancer while others die. We don't know why some children die tragically while other people live to 100. We don't know why James was killed and Peter was spared. All we know is that God knows, and that is enough for us.

There is another side to the lesson from today's reading. Sometimes, even when we are praying for a miracle, we don't believe them when they happen right in front of us. Notice that the disciples were praying intensely for Peter's release, yet, when he came to the door – in direct answer to their prayer – they didn't believe it.

So, how do we reconcile these two thoughts today? On the one hand we said that we need to leave it all up to God because sometimes good people get killed. Yet, on the other hand we see the prayers of the faithful being answered in a

Acts: The Church is Born

Session 5: Crossing the Great Divide

miraculous, resurrection-like, display of God's power. Which is it? Do we passively concede to the Sovereign will of God, or do we fervently pray in order to see God's power worked out?

The answer to this question exposes the very nature of God. The answer is...both. God calls us to pray fervently so that we will become aligned to God's will and see God's glory. Yet, it is God's will and not ours that will be done. As servants of the Almighty we need to live and pray each day holding two things in our hearts: first we need to live in expectancy that God can and will do miracles in and through us when we are available to God, and, two, it has little to do with us and everything to do with God. God is in control and we can trust God no matter what.

James died and for that we mourn. Peter was spared to preach another day, and for that we rejoice. Through it all, it is the Kingdom of God that advances, not us.

Just For Kids

Draw a picture of this story.

There are some interesting points of the story that you may want to highlight:

Herod had 16 guards watching Peter.

The angel made it so that Peter could just walk right out of the prison.

Peter thought he was dreaming at first.

The people in the house didn't believe Rhoda when she said Peter was at the door...she closed the door in his face!

How will you draw this picture?

There are two things to think about today:

1. When you pray for something, don't be surprised when it actually happens!

2. God is in control, no matter how bad the situation might seem...just keep praying!

Acts: The Church is Born

Session 5: Crossing the Great Divide

Lesson 5

Acts 12:18-24

Where did Herod make his base of operation?

What did the people of Tyre and Sidon desire from Herod? Why?

How did the people receive Herod's deliverance of peace?

How did God feel about Herod's self-opinion?

What happened to the Word of God in spite of the death of Israel's "king?"

King of the Jews

It is quite possible that today's reading may have been a bit of comic relief on the part of Luke. Please don't misunderstand; this story truly happened, to be sure. However, you can nearly taste the satirical flavor that comes through in Luke's words as he paints the portrait of Herod, king of the Jews.

For over forty years the Romans had allowed the family of King Herod the Great (the baby killer of Jesus' story) to serve as "king" over Israel. Throughout the story of the gospel these false kings had been battling the true King, Jesus, at every step.

- When Jesus was born, Joseph had to hide him in Egypt in order to save the baby from the bloodthirsty and jealous Herod the Great.
- When Jesus was in his time of ministry, it was Herod Antipas who had John beheaded and who turned Jesus over to Pilate to be executed.
- Now, as Jesus' disciples are on the move, it is the next generation of Herod, Herod Agrippa, that tried to stamp out Jesus' followers by killing James and imprisoning Peter.

Notice the beautiful irony in Luke's account of Herod's fate. The people of Tyre and Sidon came to Herod looking for peace and dependent upon him for food. Isn't that exactly what the prophets promised that the Messiah would provide in his Kingdom when it was established? Here Herod sits on the throne of Israel and proclaims in a lofty speech that he will, indeed, bring peace and provision for his people and the nations that lie around them. He will do it, and he will be happy to take the credit. Oh really? At that point Herod keels over and dies.

So, while the self-appointed and artificially induced "king of the Jews" becomes worm food, the true King of Kings, who brings peace to the world and is the bread of life, continues to expand his Kingdom.

Thanks, Luke, for the satirical reminder that we should never think of ourselves too highly than we ought and never take credit for something that only God can provide.

Acts: The Church is Born

Session 5: Crossing the Great Divide

Just For Kids

What do the phrases "pushing up daisies" or "worm food" mean?

How do those phrases apply to our story about Herod today?

Let's say that you had worked really hard on a project – like a science fair experiment, a Lego creation, or a painting. Then on the day you were supposed to present it to everyone, you were not able to make it and your brother or sister showed it to everyone. How would you feel if all the people who saw the project loved it, but they thought that your brother had made it? Then, he took all the credit for it. Do you think that would be the right thing for him to do? Why?

In our story today, that is exactly what King Herod did. He took credit for something that only God can produce – peace. Herod thought he was the King of the Jews who brought peace. Little did he know that Jesus is really the King who brings peace to the whole world.

(Footnotes)

[1] Wood, D. R. W. (1996). New Bible dictionary (3rd ed. /) (Page 153). Leicester, England; Downers Grove, Ill.: InterVarsity Press.

[2] ibid Page 50

[3] ibid Page 1154

Acts: The Church is Born

Session 6: Spreading Branches

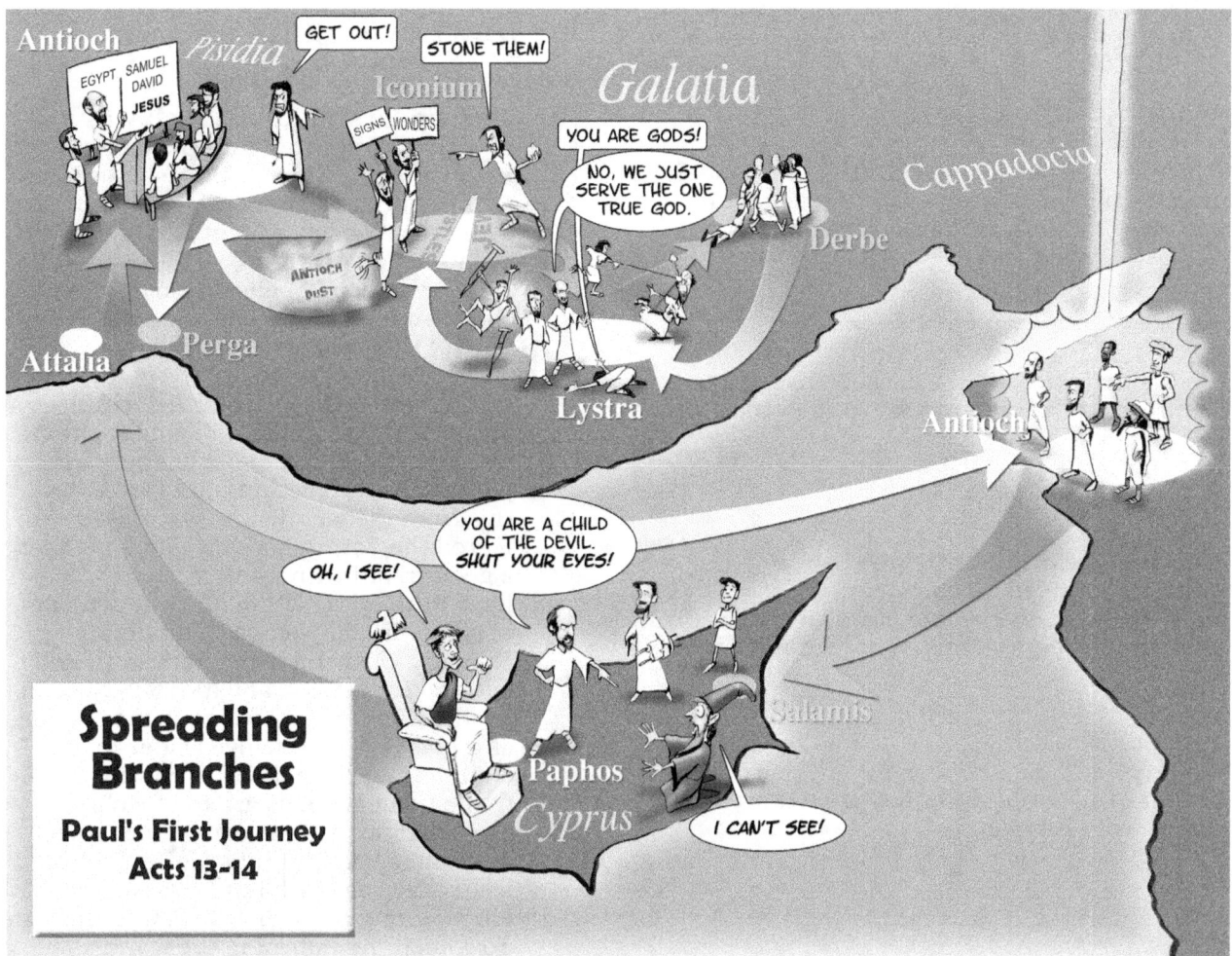

Introduction

This week we see the branches of the tree begin to spread out across the Mediterranean Sea. The seed was planted in Jerusalem. The strong trunk of a unified Israel grew as the barriers between Hebraic Jews, Grecian Jews, and Samaritans were torn down in the power of the Holy Spirit. The seed of the Kingdom crossed the great divide of nations as the Holy Spirit came upon a Roman household. Now, with a new base camp in Antioch, under the leadership of a multicultural dream team, the church launches its campaign to bring the good news of Jesus and the invitation to the Kingdom of God to the rest of the world.

This first recorded missionary journey is one that is full of intrigue, adventure, and inspiration. On the island of Cypress, Paul and Barnabas tear down the enemy's stronghold as they confront Elymas and open the door for the good news of Jesus. Then, on the mainland, in the regions of Pisidia and Galatia, Paul and Barnabas plant the first churches for Gentile nations. In this maiden voyage, we are given examples of how to confront the enemy in spiritual battle, present the gospel in culturally relevant ways, proclaim the truth, heal the sick, and keep an eternal perspective in the face of cruel opposition. These are all the essential components of any missionary endeavor, both then and now.

Acts: The Church is Born

Session 6: Spreading Branches

Lesson 1

Acts 12:25-13:12

What descriptive title was given for the leaders in Antioch? (in other words, what kind of people were they...what was their function?)

In what activities did the leaders engage during the process of appointing Saul and Barnabas?

What was the first activity that Saul and Barnabas engaged in when they landed on Cyprus (and in every other city as we will see)? Why do you suppose this activity came first?

In your own words, describe Paul's approach to dealing with Elymas.

Vv. 11-12 are a contrast of vision. What happened to Elymas' vision? What happened to Sergius' vision? Why?

What was Sergius Paulus amazed about?

The Journey Begins

Observations from this passage:

1. **The leadership of Antioch was a multicultural melting pot**. It is highly unlikely that Luke's list of leaders at the church of Antioch was a haphazard sampling. He has a point to make. Look at these men: **Barnabas** represented the core bunch of believers in Jerusalem. **Simeon** was a black man (we can deduce this because his nickname is "Niger" which is the Latin term for black). **Lucius** was a North African, and most likely of darker skin. **Manaen** was from Syrian/Hellenistic roots with political experience and ties (we deduce this from the fact that he was raised with Herod the Tetrarch and would have been a good friend with him). Finally, we have **Saul** who, within his own personal profile, was a mixed bag, combining Roman citizenship from Tarsus, Greek cultural influences, and a strong passion for the Word of God found in his training as a Pharisee. These five leaders of the church in Antioch stood in contrast to the homogeneous group of Hebraic Jews that formed the core of leaders in Jerusalem. It's not that the Jerusalem leadership was bad, but Luke was emphasizing for us that God was about to do something radical in the world so he assembled a team that was suited for the job. The Kingdom of God was no longer centered in Jerusalem and aimed only for those who were genetic descendents of Abraham; it was centered in Antioch and was now open to the entire world as it was originally intended to be.

2. **Fasting and Prayer was a key element for discernment**. Luke made sure to mention that it was in the context of a season of fasting and prayer that the leaders in Antioch were receptive to the direction of the Holy Spirit. It is when we quiet our hearts and minds through these spiritual disciplines that we will be able to hear the still small voice of the Spirit speaking into our lives.

3. **Saul adapted his presentation to the culture**. Saul did not change his name to Paul. Having been born a Roman citizen in the city of Tarsus, he would have had at least three names, each from the dominant culture of his region. Saul was his Hebrew/Jewish name. Paul was his Greek name. We

Acts: The Church is Born

Session 6: Spreading Branches

don't know his third name. When Saul moved away from Palestine, where the Christians were predominantly from a Jewish background, and started operating in primarily Greco-Roman cultures, it only made sense for him to be referred to as Paul rather than Saul. We will see throughout this study that Paul was very good at adapting his presentation to the culture in which he found himself.

4. **The stronghold must first be broken.** When Paul and Barnabas reached the island, the first thing they did was to proclaim the Word of God from the scriptures in the synagogue. That is an important example for us to follow. Paul didn't preach his word; he simply opened scripture in the synagogue and began explaining to the Jews about how Jesus had fulfilled the scriptures that they claimed to follow. Those who were open to the truth saw the logic of their arguments and came into a fuller knowledge and relationship with God.

However, there were many who, even though they read the scripture and claimed to follow them, were blinded by a distorted vision and understanding of God. Now comes the really important piece. Whenever we attempt to boldly proclaim the truth of Jesus, we will encounter a direct conflict with satanic forces. Peter experienced it when he brought the gospel to Samaria and had to deal with Simon the Magician. In today's reading we see that Paul went toe-to-toe with Elymas the Sorcerer. Notice how Elymas was identified. He was a Jewish sorcerer. In other words, he was a man who claimed to know the truth of the Torah but had blended biblical teaching with the magic arts that we discussed two weeks ago. This man had been deceived by satan to believe that God was some kind of energy or power that could be manipulated for personal gain and was being used to keep the political leader of the region in the dark. When Sergius Paulus became interested in Paul's teaching, do you think the enemy was going to stand for that? No way! He brought on a frontal attack against Paul.

Here is the lesson for today: Our enemy's only power, and his primary tactic, is to cleverly distort God's truth. Notice the approach that Paul takes in this conflict.

First, Paul takes a position of authority against the enemy; he "looked straight at Elymas."

Then, he didn't mince words, but simply identified and named the enemy at hand; "you are a child of the devil, full of deceit and trickery, perverting/distorting the right ways of the Lord."

Next, he claimed the power of God, not his own; "the hand of the Lord is against you."

Finally, he bound the enemy so that he could no longer do his work in the life of Sergius Paulus; "you will be blind."

As we progress through the study of Acts together, we will see that every time the truth of Jesus was coming into a new region there was a serious flurry of spiritual warfare. The enemy attacked Paul repeatedly. Yet, on the flip side, people were set free from spiritual oppression and delivered into the Kingdom of God. As 21st century believers, living in a society that is under the strong influence of the great deceiver, it is important for us to not lose sight of the fact that we, too, will constantly be engaged in this type of spiritual struggle. Let's follow Paul's example. We do not need to be afraid of this battle, because the victory has already been won through the death and resurrection of Jesus. We are simply soldiers on a reconnaissance mission, sent to liberate the captives and proclaim the victory! As we progress through this study, may the eyes of our enemy become dark and misty while we join Sergius Paulus and see the truth of Jesus' power for salvation in our world.

Acts: The Church is Born

Session 6: Spreading Branches

Just for Kids

Today it might be fun to make a poster of the five leaders mentioned in our reading today, but design it like a superhero poster. You could call them something like the A-Team (for Antioch team), or the Antioch 5. Have fun with it. Read the following description to base your drawings on.

> It is highly unlikely that Luke's list of leaders at the church of Antioch was a haphazard sampling. He has a point to make. Look at these men: **Barnabas** represented the core bunch of believers in Jerusalem. **Simeon** was a black man (we can deduce this because his nickname is "Niger" which is the Latin term for black). **Lucius** was a North African, and most likely of darker skin. **Manaen** was from Syrian/Hellenistic roots with political experience and ties (we deduce this from the fact that he was raised with Herod the Tetrarch and would have been a good friend with him). Finally, we have **Saul** who, within his own personal profile, was a mixed bag, combining Roman citizenship from Tarsus, Greek cultural influences, and a strong passion for the Word of God found in his training as a Pharisee. These five leaders of the church in Antioch stood in contrast to the homogeneous group of Hebraic Jews that formed the core of leaders in Jerusalem. It's not that the Jerusalem leadership was bad, but Luke was emphasizing for us that God was about to do something radical in the world so he assembled a team that was suited for the job. The Kingdom of God was no longer centered in Jerusalem and aimed only for those who were genetic descendents of Abraham, it was centered in Antioch and was now open to the entire world as it was originally intended to be.

Are all these men exactly alike? How are they different?

What does this tell you about the Kingdom of God?

Acts: The Church is Born

Session 6: Spreading Branches

Lesson 2

Acts 13:13-43

Where is the first place Paul and Barnabas went when they entered Pisidian Antioch? Why? What did they do there?

In this passage Paul delivers a gospel message that is tailor made for a Jewish audience. Let's break the message down into sections. For each section listed below, answer the question and create a basic outline. In the end, try to determine Paul's line of reasoning.

vv. 17-22 What are the key historical events that Paul highlights leading up to King David?

vv. 23-25 What role did John the Baptist play in the process?

vv. 26-37 How is Jesus presented?

In what way was the promise to Abraham fulfilled? (v. 33)

vv. 38-41 What promise is made? What warning is given?

How do the people respond to Paul's message?

The Message for Jews

Today we see an example of the normal pattern of Paul's mission to a new city. The first thing he would do is go directly to the local synagogue and engage in regular worship there. It was common practice in the synagogues that whenever there was a visiting rabbi (teacher) present, the elders of that synagogue would invite him to bring the message from the scripture reading for that day. This happened to Jesus when he was in the synagogue in his hometown of Nazareth. Paul, being a Jewish rabbi from the tradition of the Pharisees, would naturally accept the offer to preach. Thus, he would begin with the scripture of the day, and move into the sweeping story of the Old Testament and how the whole story points to the person of Jesus Christ.

The important thing to note today is that the crux of his message was not merely centered on the person of Jesus Christ, but, more exactly, on the resurrection of Jesus. From the beginning of the Old Testament story, God had made a promise to Abraham that, through his family, all nations would be blessed. Up until the coming of Jesus, the nation of Israel had done very little to bless the world. In fact, they had blocked out the world and condemned it to hell. Had Jesus been just another rabbi with some nice ideas about world peace there would be nothing to talk about. The center of the good news of Jesus is that he died for the sins of the world and, more importantly, rose from the dead as a demonstration of God's power over sin and death. Now that Jesus is eternally resurrected, there can be a true King on the throne of God's Kingdom and the doors can be thrown open for the whole world to enter into God's grace, forgiveness, reconciliation, and peace.

As we share this good news in our world, let's never forget one simple fact. We are not teachers of a new philosophy, we are simply witnesses to the fact that Jesus rose from the dead. In that resurrection power, we, too, can overcome the effects of sin and death in our lives and live in the fullness of life today and the assurance of life eternal.

Acts: The Church is Born

Session 6: Spreading Branches

Just for Kids

When Paul preached about Jesus to the Jews in Pisidian Antioch he told the quick history of the Old Testament first. Why do you think he did that?

Here are the key characters that he mentioned. See how much you know about each one. Where would you go to learn more about each one?

    Israelites in Egypt

    Wandering in the desert

    Judges

    Samuel

    Saul (the king, not the apostle)

    David

According to vv. 30-33, what is the most important part of Jesus' story? Why?

Make up a cheer that tells how important the resurrection is for salvation.

Acts: The Church is Born

Session 6: Spreading Branches

Lesson 3

Acts 13:44-14:7

Vv. 44-50. Summarize the conflict between Paul and the Jews.

Read Luke 9:1-5 and Luke 10:1-12. In what ways is Paul following Jesus' instructions in these passages?

How did the Lord confirm the message of grace that Paul and Barnabas preached?

Summarize the events that happened in Iconium.

How did Paul and Barnabas respond to the opposition?

Expect Opposition

Yesterday we saw a wonderful example of Paul's standard message to the Jews. The Jews were (and are) a blessed people because they have had the direct revelation of the one true God from the beginning of their history. They had been waiting and anticipating the coming of the Messiah for generations. When presented with the clear truth of Jesus' resurrection and his position as the Messiah and the Son of God, many, many of them made the natural transition from being an Old Testament Jew to being a New Testament Jew as they simply accepted Jesus as the long awaited Messiah.

Many, however, after hearing the same message, did not receive this message warmly. Here is the lesson for us today: Anytime the gospel is presented it is going to polarize a crowd. Those whose hearts are ready will come toward the healing light of the good news. Those whose hearts are calloused and are riddled with the twisted roots of the distorted truth, will become hostile to the truth and work with a vengeance to see the preaching of the good news get shut down.

There are many reasons for this resistance. Some who are in leadership of the local system fear losing control and feel compelled to squash the competition. Others may have invested great amounts of money into the current religious system and are afraid of losing their fiscal viability if the status quo is upset. Still others may be under the direct control of satan and, having their minds darkened by a syncretistic folk religion, are under orders to destroy the proclaimers of Jesus' good news.

As followers of Jesus we need to be prepared for this mixed reception. Being a proclaimer of Jesus is probably not going to win you a popularity contest. More than likely it may cost you your job or reputation. It may even cost you your life. Yet, when you consider the true healing and transformation that will come to those who embrace the good news and step into the healing and transforming power of God's grace, then the opposition fades into an irrelevant issue in the eternal perspective.

As we fight the fight and proclaim the truth, let us never give up hope. "Let us fix our eyes on Jesus, the author and perfecter of our faith, who for the joy set before him endured the cross, scorning its shame, and sat down at the right hand of the throne of God. Consider him who endured such opposition from sinful men, so that you will not grow weary and lose heart." (Hebrews 12:2-3)

Acts: The Church is Born

Session 6: Spreading Branches

Just for Kids

It's map time again. Get out your maps and chart Paul and Barnabas' journey in chs. 13-14. Here are the major cities to plot.

Antioch (beginning point)
Seleucia
Salamis
Paphos
Perga
Antioch in Pisidia
Iconium
Lystra
Derbe
Attalia

Draw arrows to indicate Paul and Barnabas' journey.

Acts: The Church is Born

Session 6: Spreading Branches

Lesson 4

Acts 14:8-20

When Paul and Barnabas entered Pisidian Antioch (13:14) and Iconium (14:1) what the first thing they did?

What was the first thing they did in Lystra? What does this tell you about the population of Lystra?

How did the crowd respond to the miracle of healing?

In vv. 15-17 we find the first gospel message to a completely non-Jewish audience. Compare this message to the message preached to the Jews in Pisidian Antioch (13:13-43) In what ways does Paul change his approach for this new audience?

Who upset the crowd in Lystra and turned them against Paul? Why?

How did Paul respond to the fact that he was stoned and left for dead?

The Message for Gentiles

In this first missionary journey we are given examples of the two types of approach when presenting the good news of Jesus. In Lesson 2 we saw how Paul presented the good news to the Jews. He started with scripture and their current theological understanding and built a logical argument from the scripture as to why Jesus was the long-awaited Messiah. With the Jews he could do this because he shared a common cultural heritage with them and was able to make natural connections to images and ideas that totally registered with their worldview.

In today's reading we witness the first truly pagan encounter. There were obviously no synagogues in Lystra because Luke does not tell us that Paul went there first to preach. The absence of a synagogue means that Lystra was entirely populated by Greco-Roman people who knew nothing of the Hebrew scriptures and were most likely fully engulfed in the worship of a pagan god or a pantheon of deities.

Here are some observations from Paul's cross-cultural missions experience that will help us as we interact with the "unchurched" in our daily lives, and with the cross-cultural experiences that you may get to have in your life.

1. **It begins with power**. Please don't misunderstand. It doesn't begin with a big showy display of theatrics or an overture of dominance, either politically or ideologically. The power, in this case, is the power of God to bring healing to broken lives. When Jesus sent the disciples on their training missions during his ministry, he sent them with three objectives: Teach about the Kingdom, heal the sick, and cast out demons. When you come into a culture (whether it is your atheistic neighbor or the village in Africa) that has no common context in the Scripture with you, then it is vital that they see a demonstration of the healing power of God's love at work through your life. There are many people selling things in our world. There are a lot of talkers. People, in our culture especially, aren't really listening to words anymore. What they need to see is action. They need to see unconditional love. They need to see authority over the darkness that controls their lives. They need to see fear, doubt, and sickness driven out from their presence and the miraculous power of God demonstrated before their eyes. When they see this, being carried out by a simple, humble, servant of Jesus, then they may... may...be willing to listen.

2. **Meet them where they are.** Paul was the master of meeting people at a common

Acts: The Church is Born

Session 6: Spreading Branches

place and beginning with language that would make sense to their worldview. When he spoke with Jews he reasoned from the scripture and spoke of the resurrected Messiah. When he spoke with the Greeks who thought he was a god he spoke of the God above all gods who created all things and gives grace to all people. As ambassadors for Jesus we must always remember to respect and understand the worldview of the person to whom we are speaking and trying to communicate the transcendent truth of Jesus in words that will connect.

3. **Expect opposition.** Many of us in the American Evangelical church have grown dull in our experience of the power of God. We may have even lost faith that God can and does even work through God's people like God did in Acts. When we honestly read this book and allow ourselves to become excited about the potential power that we could experience when we trust in God, we can get lulled into an equally disabling lie. We can believe that if we have enough faith then God will work (and must) work great miracles through us and that all people will flock to us and we will do great things for God's Kingdom. Keep in mind one thing. While it is true that you can do great things for God's Kingdom and that great ministry can, and will, happen through you, that does not mean that you are suddenly going to have a stress free and happy-go-lucky life. When you start boldly proclaiming God's truth and lives are being changed, then you had better believe that the enemies attack will come on harder than ever. You need not look any farther than Paul's life to know the truth of this statement. With all the great things that God did through the vessel of Paul, he was never without violent enemies who sought to kill him at every turn. Eventually they did kill him. So, before you run into battle, remember Jesus' words "If anyone comes to me and does not hate his father and mother, his wife and children, his brothers and sisters—yes, even his own life—he cannot be my disciple. And anyone who does not carry his cross and follow me cannot be my disciple.

"Suppose one of you wants to build a tower. Will he not first sit down and estimate the cost to see if he has enough money to complete it? For if he lays the foundation and is not able to finish it, everyone who sees it will ridicule him, saying, 'This fellow began to build and was not able to finish.'"(Luke 14:26-30)

Just for Kids

Have you ever studied Greek mythology? If so, who were Zeus and Hermes?

If you haven't studied these Greek gods, read the following:

Zeus -- the chief deity of the Greek pantheon, often described as 'the father of gods and men.' Zeus as the 'sky god,' who wielded the thunder bolt and was responsible for weather and rain while enthroned on Mount Olympus, was of Indo-European origin. By Homeric times (ca. 800 B.C.) Zeus was the highest civic god, protector of justice and morals. The circle of twelve gods and goddesses established as a family on Olympus is evident in Homer. Other elements in the Zeus mythology appear to have had a different origin. Zeus's father, Kronos, was said to have swallowed his children until he was given a stone instead of Zeus, which also freed other gods of Zeus's generation, Hera, Poseidon, and Hades. Other features of the Zeus legend include the overthrow of the earlier generation, the Titanc, 'sons of Earth,' and the unions with various goddesses and mortal women.

In Hellenistic times (ca. 300 B.C.-A.D. 300) Zeus was identified with the chief deity of any non-Greek religion. The Stoics spoke of the highest principle, fire or reason, which animates the universe, as 'Zeus.' Barnabas is taken to be 'Zeus' by the people of Lystra (Acts 14:12).[1]

Hermes The divine messenger of the Greek gods. Originally a demon that haunted the piles of stones set up as roadside markers, Hermes was the messenger of the greater gods, especially Zeus. He was also a trickster who stole Apollo's cattle and was thought to have invented the lyre. Paul and Barnabas are mistaken for Hermes and Zeus when they visit Lystra and Paul heals a cripple there (Acts 14:12).[2]

How does Paul teach the people about God (vv. 15-17)? Does he use the Bible? Why or why not?

The lesson for today is to remember that it is possible to talk to people about God that may have never read the Bible before. God's greatness can be seen in the wonders of creation. Many times it is good to start sharing with people about God by talking about creation and the fact that there must be a creator who is above all the things that have been created. When a person realizes that there must be one ultimate God, then you can share with them what the Bible has to say about God and God's plan of salvation that comes through Jesus.

Acts: The Church is Born

Session 6: Spreading Branches

Lesson 5

Acts 14:21-28

Where did they travel in v. 21? Why? Keeping in mind the events that took place in those cities, how do you think Paul and Barnabas were received in those cities?

What was the message of "encouragement" that Paul delivered to the disciples? Do you find this encouraging? Why or why not?

Read the following passages. How does Paul describe his life?

> 2 Corinthians 6:3-10 and 11:22-33.

What did Paul and Barnabas leave in each church? Why?

How was this decision made?

What did Paul and Barnabas do when they returned to Antioch?

In vv. 26-27 how does Luke describe the purpose of the mission that had just been completed?

Leaving churches, leaving leaders

Here are two thoughts for today:

1. **Hardships are part of the package.** Yesterday we ended on an intense note. The christian life is an intense one that is full of battles. It is not for the timid or the weak. As you read Paul's autobiographies in 2 Corinthians 6 and 11, there was, most likely, a sick feeling in the pit of your stomach, wondering if you could endure such things. The irony of this passage is that Paul's words, "We must go through many hardships to enter the kingdom of God" were intended to be an encouragement. If we could just break into the perspective that Paul had, then we, too, would be able to see them as such. Read his words that he wrote to the church in Philippi,

    > " I rejoice greatly in the Lord that at last you have renewed your concern for me. Indeed, you have been concerned, but you had no opportunity to show it. I am not saying this because I am in need, for I have learned to be content whatever the circumstances. I know what it is to be in need, and I know what it is to have plenty. I have learned the secret of being content in any and every situation, whether well fed or hungry, whether living in plenty or in want. I can do everything through him who gives me strength." (Philippians 4:10-13, NIV)

2. **It is important to have spiritual leaders.** When Paul planted a church he was leaving behind a group of young and vulnerable believers. The best analogy for the church in this instance is to remember Jesus' words when he said we were his sheep (John 10). Paul and Barnabas created a herd of sheep and left them behind, knowing that they were surrounded by ravenous wolves who would like nothing better than to tear this fledgling flock to shreds. In order to protect these young churches it was vital that they leave behind godly men who would be able to guide and protect the church in the generations to come.

    If you would like to learn more about the role of an elder in the local church, read the following passages. These passages were written for the men mentioned in

Acts: The Church is Born

Session 6: Spreading Branches

today's stories, and they are instructive for our churches as well.

> 1 Timothy 3:1-7
>
> 1 Timothy 5:17-19
>
> Titus 1:5-16
>
> James 5:14
>
> 1 Peter 5:1-11

Spend some time today praying for the elders in your church. Do you know who they are? Do you know how to specifically pray for them? Do you realize that they are major targets for the enemy's attacks? This is true because of the old saying, "strike the shepherd, scatter the sheep." Pray that the elders would be in submission to God, committed to prayer and fasting, and open to the leading and power of the Holy Spirit.

Just for Kids

On this first missionary journey, Paul started a new church in every city that he visited. Before he left those brand new churches he established a group of leaders, called "elders," in each community to take care of the church.

Do you know who the elders are in your church?

The elders are the men who are responsible for taking care of the people in your church and making sure that everyone loves God, learning from the Bible, praying for each other, taking care of each other, and taking care of the poor and needy. It's a big job.

Spend some time today writing a little note of encouragement to your elders. They'd really appreciate it.

(Footnotes)

[1] Achtemeier, P. J., Harper & Row, P., & Society of Biblical Literature. (1985). *Harper's Bible dictionary*. Includes index. (1st ed.) (Page 1163). San Francisco: Harper & Row.

[2] ibid. (Page 384).

Acts: The Church is Born

Session 7: Moving Into Greece

Introduction

In the introduction to this study, there was a chart that showed a big tree. At the top of the trunk there were a few small branches that began to grow, but then they all merged together in a giant clot. This week we examine the clot. A great controversy broke out in the city of Antioch. The Jewish Christians were having a very difficult time accepting the fact that uncircumcised Gentiles were being welcomed into the family of God with no regard for the Law of Moses. These "concerned citizens" took matters into their own hands and began teaching the Antiochians that they must be circumcised in order to be "truly saved." This controversy forced, what we call, the first church council. The council was the clot. The decision of this council allowed absolute freedom for the church to spread open its branches for the whole world to see.

In the wake of this liberation, Paul sets out on his second missionary journey and discovers that God has plans for him that were not at all part of Paul's original agenda. Being sensitive to the leading of the Holy Spirit, Paul ventures north and crosses over into Alexander the Great's old romping ground: Macedonia. This week and next we will discover the great work that God has in store for Paul among the Greeks.

Acts: The Church is Born

Session 7: Moving Into Greece

Lesson 1

Acts 15:1-35

What was the main issue that caused the leaders to gather in Jerusalem?

Briefly summarize the two sides of the debate.

What was Peter's argument?

What was Paul and Barnabas' argument?

What was James' conclusion?

Concerning Conflict

Here are two observations from today's reading:

1. **People like to squabble.** From its inception, the church has been fraught with controversy. In Acts 15 we see the first real controversy within the church. For centuries, the Jews had believed that God would save the world through the Jewish nation. In their interpretation of God's promise of blessing to the nations, all nations would convert to Judaism, be circumcised, and follow the Levitical code of Moses' Law. Then, after everyone looked exactly the same, the world would be at peace. So, naturally, the Pharisees in Jerusalem who accepted the fact that the resurrected Jesus of Nazareth was, indeed, the long awaited Messiah, assumed that the path to knowing the Messiah was through the gateway of Judaism. Please forgive the caricature on the chart which paints these "Judaizers" as evil "snippers" who are villainous in nature. (although Paul may have felt that way at times) The truth is that they were probably well meaning Christ-followers who had not yet fully realized the vastness of God's grace and were, understandably, operating under their worldview of origin.

    In our churches today we see the same things happening. Each of us has been raised in some type of theological environment. Whether we were raised as a child in this environment, or have had our imprinting conversion experience in an environment, that theological perspective will always feel like home to us. It will feel the most right and natural. Unfortunately, just like in marriage, when Christ-followers come together in fellowship, but are coming from different "home-bases" of theological perspective, it can lead to conflict. Sometimes, as we see in Antioch, the dispute can become intense and cause sharp division among the church.

2. **The rule is love and unity in the name of Jesus.** The lesson of Acts 15 can be found in the decision that the "council" came to after hearing all the evidence. Peter said, "Look, Cornelius was unclean, but the Spirit came on him." Paul and Barnabas were witnesses

Acts: The Church is Born

Session 7: Moving Into Greece

to the signs and wonders that God had done among the Gentiles. It is obvious that God's plan is bigger than any one group's theological preference and perspective. God is at work in the world, in spite of our narrow-mindedness, rigidity, legalistic tendencies, and ethnocentricity. Our job is to be open to it, observe what the Spirit of God is actually doing, and join him there.

At first glance, the letter to Antioch may appear to run counter to the openness of the decision that the council concluded, in that it gives a set of rules for the church to follow. Yet, with proper inspection, we can see that the letter actually tells us the heart of the message.

> *The rules' specifics and their rationale (Acts 15:21) show they are given to promote table fellowship between uncircumcised Gentile converts and Jewish Christians who observe the dietary laws. There is no surrender here of the gospel freedom alluded to in verse 19. Rather, that freedom is to be used in love to serve Jewish Christian brothers and sisters, but not beyond the bounds of Scripture (Gal 5:13). Sexual immorality, as an ethical matter, not having to do with ritual purity, may seem out of place. But given that one of the Jews' ongoing concerns was "low ethical and moral standards among Gentiles" (Scott 1992:14), it is appropriate in this list to represent the category of moral standards.*
>
> *James' proposal, then, teaches us three things about life together in a culturally diverse church. We must say no to any form of cultural imperialism that demands others' conformity to our cultural standards before we will accept them and their spiritual experience. We must say yes to mutual respect for our differences. And we must live out that respect even to the extent of using our freedom to forgo what is permissible in other circumstances.*
>
> *In a day when transportation and urbanization make it easier to stay apart than face the challenge of living together as a multicultural body of believers, the church has yet to model consistently what James calls for. But even our separate culturally homogeneous fellowships may face challenges of gender, music and generation gaps. We need to take Acts 15 to heart.*[1]

Are there any areas of theology or doctrinal distinctives that you find to be inhibiting your fellowship in your church? Spend some time asking God to expose to you where you may be displaying some legalism or drawing some unnecessary distinctions. On the other hand, if you feel a sense of freedom to do certain things because of grace and freedom in Christ, but you know that those things will become a stumbling block to someone else, ask God to show you how you could be more considerate to your brother or sister and not do those things out of love for them. Let's not let secondary issues inhibit the unity of the body and the overflow of God's Kingdom!

(If this topic strikes a chord with you, refer to Paul's teaching in 1 Corinthians 8)

Just for Kids

Has your family ever gotten into an argument over something in which two people disagreed about how something should be done? What was it? How did you handle it?

In the story today, the Christians in Jerusalem and Antioch got in a big fight about whether Gentile (non-Jewish) Christians should have to follow Moses' Law or not. In the story, we see a good model for how to handle arguments.

1. Don't yell, talk calmly.
2. Listen to everyone's side of the story before you make decisions.
3. Come to a compromise where everybody can win.

In this story the Jewish Christians didn't "win" the argument, but, out of love for them, the Gentiles agreed that they would not eat certain kind of foods so that they would actually be able to eat at the same dinner table without anybody getting upset.

The point is that we should always place the other person higher than ourselves and try to find a way to demonstrate love them, even when we are arguing.

Acts: The Church is Born

Session 7: Moving Into Greece

Lesson 2

Acts 15:36-16:5

What issue came between Paul and Barnabas? What were your reactions when you first read this? Why?

What is Timothy's ethnic background?

What does Paul do to Timothy? Why?

In light of the decisions made in Jerusalem in chapter 15, why do you suppose Paul did this to Timothy?

Leaving Barnabas, Finding Timothy

Leaving Barnabas

There is a positive side and a negative side to this story. The negative side is obvious. It is always discouraging when people disagree and split company. Barnabas and Paul had been partners for a long time. Barnabas was Paul's first friend. When Paul first came to Jesus, and no one would accept his conversion as authentic, Barnabas was there to be his friend and advocate. Paul and Barnabas were teaching partners in the ministry at Antioch. They were the first to go out across the sea and spread the Good News of the Kingdom of God to Gentiles in the greater Roman Empire. Now, two friends are torn apart because of a difference of opinion. It is sad.

Yet, on the positive side, we can take comfort in the fact that two spiritual giants like Paul and Barnabas were still human, like us. Isn't it ironic that, in the wake of the Jerusalem Council, just after the message of unity in the body of Christ was proclaimed, Paul and Barnabas disagree so sharply that they can no longer work together.

We must remember that each of us is on a path of development. As we discussed yesterday, we each have theological biases and ecclesiological hobby-horses and soap boxes upon which we love to stand. The ultimate goal is that we can all set these things aside and live in the freedom of God's grace and the love that Jesus called us to share with each other (even our enemies). Yet, we aren't there yet. Sometimes, there does come a time when two people will find that their differences are so strong that they cannot work side by side. So, Paul takes Silas back to Galatia and Barnabas takes John Mark back to Cyprus.

Here is an evidence of the grace of God at work. Even though this disagreement was not exemplary of God's desire and design for God's church, God still could use it and work God's will and God's Kingdom through it. When Paul and Barnabas split up, the mission work was doubled. Now there were two groups moving in the world instead of one. God will use us in spite of our petty humanness. Praise God! In the end, we must remember, Paul, Barnabas, and John Mark were reconciled. Perhaps Paul was humbled and came down off his high horse. Or, perhaps John Mark repented and made things right regarding his issues that led to his abandonment of Paul. In any case, unity and

Acts: The Church is Born

Session 7: Moving Into Greece

reconciliation was ultimately achieved. We are in process. Let's be patient with one another.

Finding Timothy

There is great irony in this story. Paul had just come from the Jerusalem Council where it had been decided that Gentiles did not have to be circumcised in order to be saved. He had also written the letter to the Galatians in which he speaks very strongly concerning the same matter and elaborates that we have freedom in Christ that is apart from the Law. It is all about walking in the Spirit and bearing the fruit of the Spirit that matters. Whether a man has a foreskin or doesn't has no bearing whatsoever on his place in the Kingdom of God. And then, he meets young Timothy and circumcises him.

What is up with that? Why did Paul feel the need to circumcise Timothy when, as we will see later, he does not circumcise Titus?

Timothy was a bi-racial boy. His mother was Jewish and his father was Greek. You can just guess how the Jewish community felt about this little boy – how they felt about his mother. He was a disgrace to them and they would have nothing to do with him. So Paul circumcised him in order to remove unnecessary hindrances to the mission.

Here is an important point that is at the heart of Paul's theology. In 1 Corinthians 12:23-24 Paul said, "Everything is permissible"—but not everything is beneficial. "Everything is permissible"—but not everything is constructive. Nobody should seek his own good, but the good of others." *Everything* is permissible. Do you hear that? That is freedom in Christ. Whether you have a foreskin or not; whether you observe certain festivals or not; whether you eat certain foods or not; whether you go to movies or not – all of these things are simply things. They are not unclean or clean, they simply are. Jesus said that it is not what goes into a man that makes him unclean, but what comes out of his heart that makes him clean or unclean.

So, in light of this theology, Paul didn't have a problem with circumcising Timothy and not circumcising Titus. It didn't really matter. Yet, out of love for people and a desire for unity and the bond of peace, he was willing to meet the people of that region where they were and work with them there.

Just for Kids

Take a piece of paper and hold it up. This paper is one nice piece. You could probably draw a really great picture on it.

Now tear the paper in half in a rough way, not with a nice crease, but with a big ripping motion. What does it look now? Is it still useful as a whole paper? Can you still draw on each half?

Tape the pieces back together. Try to match the tears closely.

What is the paper like after you taped it? Is it as good as new? Can it still be used?

The lesson for today is that conflict can be very destructive to your family and to the church. Once you tear yourself away from someone, it leaves a big mark and does damage. Even if the damage is taped back together, it still leaves a scar.

Let's work hard at working out our conflict and not splitting up like Paul and Barnabas did.

Acts: The Church is Born

Session 7: Moving Into Greece

Lesson 3

Acts 16:6-10

From what regions was Paul kept from traveling? Why?

Through what means were God's orders communicated to Paul?

How did Paul respond to the calling?

Use your map to see the areas through which Paul traveled (and wasn't allowed to travel) and the region to which he was called. What is significant about the region to which he was called?

Notice the voice of the passage (first person, third person, etc.). In what way does the voice change? Why?

Divine Detours

Have you ever had a plan that you thought was from God, that you thought made total sense, and that would bring glory to God and effectiveness to ministry...and then it flopped? In our story today, we are confronted with one of the most difficult aspects of following God and serving in God's Kingdom. When Paul left the region in which he had planted churches during his first missionary trip, he set off for the west in order to expand the work of planting churches. The trajectory he was on (heading into Asia) leads us to believe that he was intent upon arriving in Ephesus. This makes sense. If you were going to start a vital, church-planting ministry, where would you choose to go? Where would be the most strategic location from which to launch a region-wide campaign for the expansion of God's Kingdom? You would want to find a cosmopolitan hub of trade and travel from which you could make the most dramatic impact for God. Right? Of course you would, and so would Paul. That is what Ephesus was; it was the hub of Asia. Ephesus would have been the ideal place to do ministry.

But God had a different plan. God said, "No, Paul, you aren't going to Asia, I want you to go to Troas." "Troas!?!" Paul must have thought. "Why would I want to go to Troas? Troas is way to the north. It isn't a regional hub; it's a way station for people who are on a land-route to Rome. I thought I was going to reach Asia."

"Go to Troas. You'll figure it out when you get there." "Yes, Lord."

In Troas, Paul had a vision of a Macedonian man calling him to come over. Macedonia. This was a place that was as pagan as they came. It was here that Alexander the Great grew up and from here that he conquered the world with Greek culture. Now, under the rule of the Roman Empire, it was a vacation spot for the Roman upper class. There were very few Jews in the region. Paul had never considered this place. Hmmm...Macedonia. That could work.

Here's the lesson for us: It is OK to make big plans for God. Make you plans, set out on your course and set the goals to accomplish those plans. But, in the going, be careful. Make sure that your plans do not become your god. As you are traveling toward your desired destination, always be listening to the still, soft voice of the Spirit. Be aware of the spiritual roadblocks and detour signs. Not every obstacle that lies in your path is from the enemy. The roadblock on the way to Ephesus was divinely placed in order to help Paul broaden his perspective. When you

Acts: The Church is Born

Session 7: Moving Into Greece

hear the voice, be willing to bag your plans and get with God's plan. Always hold your objectives with open hands, realizing that God is the director of the course.

Just for Kids

Today is another map day.

Read through chapter 16 and plot out the regions and cities through which Paul traveled.

Where did Paul want to go? Where did God tell him to go?

How do you think Paul felt when he didn't get to do what he wanted to do?

Have you ever had a time when you really wanted to do something but your parents said you had to do something else? How did you feel?

Paul knew that God, who is his Father, knew better than he did and knew what was best for him. So, Paul did not whine or pout about it, he simply said, "Yes, Lord" and obeyed.

The next time your parents want you to do something, remember that they love you and want the best for you. Trust them, and simply obey. Whining will just make it miserable.

Acts: The Church is Born
Session 7: Moving Into Greece

Lesson 4

Acts 16:11-24

What was special about Philippi?

Where did they go in Philippi and what did they expect to find there?

What kind of people gathered there? How did they respond to the Gospel?

How did the spirit respond to Paul and Silas? Why? Read Luke 4:31-37. Are there any parallels with this story from Jesus' ministry?

What upset the girl's owners?

How were Paul and Silas treated for delivering the girl from the power of an evil spirit? Why?

Welcome Luke

Did you notice that the voice of the narrative switch from the third person ("they") to the first person ("we")? That means that in Troas, Luke joins Paul's traveling party. From this point on in the story of Acts, Luke tells Paul's story from an eyewitness perspective. It is important to stop, just for a moment, and realize the importance of this event. Luke is the author of the Gospel of Luke and the book of Acts. It is through his pen that we learn about the angels that visit Mary and the shepherds, the life and teaching of Jesus, and the Holy Spirit's activities at Pentecost. All of these events took place in Jerusalem and Palestine, yet Luke was from Troas. How did he learn these things?

There are two things to note about Luke and his history and theology.

1. His theological "imprinting" comes from Paul. In a sense, we could consider the Gospel of Luke and the book of Acts (up to this point) as the gospel according to Paul as it was taught to Luke.

2. Later in the story we will discover that Paul was imprisoned in Caesarea for two years. During that time he most likely spent time in Jerusalem and Palestine, investigating the stories that Paul had told him about regarding the life of Jesus and the early church.

Another Spiritual Battle

Today we catch another installment of one of the running themes in Acts. Whenever the gospel came to a new region it was confronted with direct spiritual warfare. The same is true today. Satan rules in the hearts of people. Do you remember when Jesus was tempted? Satan offered to hand over all the kingdoms to Jesus if he would simply bow down to him. Jesus did not correct satan for having a distorted self-understanding. He knew that satan was indeed the prince of this world (John 12:31; 14:30; 16:11; Ephesians 2:2; 6:12). Satan's greatest desire is to keep people's hearts and minds bound down by distorted thinking so that they will not be able to see the light of truth that shines through Jesus Christ and the Kingdom of God that he brought to reclaim the world. So, whenever the message of Jesus is brought into a new territory, there is going to be a battle.

The battle in Philippi took place in the life of a young girl. She had a spirit through which she could predict the future. The really interesting thing about the demonic encounters, both in

Acts: The Church is Born

Session 7: Moving Into Greece

Acts and the gospels, is how willing the demons are to proclaim the truth about Jesus. Compare this to the story in Luke 4. Here's a key principle: The demons, being spiritual creatures and seeing with spiritual eyes, know exactly who Jesus is. They see him in all his glory as the eternal ruler. After all, Jesus created them and was their loving leader in the beginning. Yet they have rebelled against him and desperately seek to undermine him and destroy the beauty that he has created.

This little girl was a pawn in a twisted game. Her owners were using her "magic" to make a boat load of money. The people in the region (representing all of us, really) were desperately seeking to tap into the mysteries of life and know if there was hope and direction for them. They were willing to pay money to have this "gifted" child tell them what to expect.

Here's a thought. This is just a speculation for the purpose of thinking outside the box…please understand. Have you ever wondered why the spirit proclaimed the truth about Paul and Silas if he was intent on undermining Jesus' mission? Why not lie, or at least keep his mouth shut. What if this spirit's job was simply to speak the truth about whomever it encountered? After all, it did tell people's fortunes, right? When Fred would come in contact with the spirit, it would proclaim "Look at Fred, he's a big fat loser, and his wife is about to dump him!" Next in line, the local banker would come to the spirit, and the spirit would proclaim, "Look everybody, here's Bill, and he's cheating you on your interest." This spirit's function was to simply thrust your "stuff" into the public light, for good or bad. Then Paul comes on the scene, the spirit sees him and proclaims, "Hey, look, everybody, here are servants of the Most High God, who will tell you how to be saved!" That was the truth, right? Paul allowed this to happen for many days, until he became troubled with it and told the spirit to take a hike.

Not all "evil" spirits are dastardly, gargoylish imps intent on tearing your flesh apart. Some spirits are simply performing the function for which they were created –by God, remember. In fact, they may even be very friendly. But here's the dangerous part, they are evil because they are not functioning in submission to God's plan. They are under the leadership of the prince of this world.

Here are the two sins in this situation, as I see it, and the heart of the spiritual battle that Paul had to fight. First, there was a renegade spirit who was in rebellion against God and using his God-given purpose in a self-serving manner that was separated from God's plan. Second, there was an abuse and an exploitation of a little girl for the sole purpose of profit. Humans are not property to be owned, and spiritual insight is not a parlor trick to be used for profit. Everything in the universe, both spiritual and physical, was created by God and is designed to be used in accordance with God's plan. If it is not, then it is corrupted and needs to be redeemed.

Just for Kids

Have you ever seen a movie or read in your history books about how children were treated at the turn of the 20th century in the United States. Millions of children were forced to work long hours in factories while the business owners got rich. Do you think that was right? How does it make you feel?

In our story today a young girl was being abused just like that. She was a slave and her owners were using her to make a lot of money through the spirit that lived inside her.

Jesus set her free from the spirit and from her owners.

There are many children in the world today who are being abused in similar ways. Spend some time praying for these children and ask God to help them find freedom.

Acts: The Church is Born

Session 7: Moving Into Greece

Lesson 5

Acts 16:25-40

How did Paul and Silas handle being beaten and thrown in jail? Why?

What surprised the jailer?

How did Paul explain the process of being saved? How is this the same or different from other encounters so far in Acts (The Samaritans, The Ethiopian Eunuch, Cornelius, etc.)?

What caused the magistrates to be alarmed regarding Paul?

A True Miracle

Another running theme in the book of Acts is the fact that God used signs and wonders to proclaim God's Kingdom in the world. In today's story there is another evidence of this. There was a miracle in Philippi that night. This miracle demonstrated the power of God to a Roman jailer, so much so that he and his entire household were saved. What was the miracle? Was it the mighty earthquake that shook the prison's foundations and set the captives free? No. That wasn't the miracle. After all, earthquakes happen all the time and the skeptic can rationalize the earthquake away as a simple natural coincidence.

There were two miracles that night that led the jailer to salvation. The first miracle is found in v. 25. Even after Paul and Silas had been brutally beaten by a Roman jailer, and had been unjustly thrown in prison, they were praying and singing hymns! In the face of the worst possible physical circumstances, those who are operating within the Kingdom of God will be able to rise above the storm and see the good in it. They will be able to praise God in all things. That is a miracle.

The second miracle is the fact that, after the chains had been loosened and the gates flung open, Paul and Silas did not escape! Anyone who was functioning under the power of the flesh and the kingdom of man would have become opportunists at that point and high-tailed it to the hills when they saw the open prison doors. Not Paul and Silas. These two men of God did not see a terrible situation and an opportunity to save their own skin. Instead, they were other-oriented, and they saw a man who was truly afraid for his life, gripped by the fear and the pressure of his job, and so lost that he was ready to take his own life. This was the man who had beaten them earlier that night. A normal man would have been glad that the jailer was about to plunge a sword into his own heart. But not Paul and Silas. The love of Jesus poured out and overflowed from them so that they could say to the jailer, "Don't harm yourself, we're all here." That is a miracle.

When the jailer saw the powerful difference that Jesus made in the lives of these men, he knew that he needed what they had. It wasn't their condemnation of him that brought him to salvation. It was their bright light of demonstrating the faith and love of God that exposed the darkness in the jailer's heart and drew him into the desire to seek salvation.

May we be that kind of miracle in the lives of the people we meet this week.

Acts: The Church is Born

Session 7: Moving Into Greece

Just for Kids

Let's have some fun and act out the story.

Here are the parts of the story. Act them out how you like.

- The jailer beats Paul and Silas (remember, this is acting…don't hurt anybody)
- Paul and Silas are locked up in chains in jail.
- Have Paul and Silas be in chains singing and praying.
- Earthquake!!!
- When the jailer sees the doors open he tries to kill himself.
- Paul and Silas say that there is no need to harm himself because they are still there.
- The jailer asks how to be saved.
- The jailer cleans Paul and Silas up and they share a meal together.

If you were in prison, do you think you would be able to sing and have a good attitude?

The next time you feel like life is hard, remember Paul and Silas in jail. Life is good when we choose to see it through God's eyes and not through our own.

(Footnotes)

[1] Larkin, W. J., Briscoe, D. S., & Robinson, H. W. (1995). *Vol. 5: Acts*. The IVP New Testament commentary series (Ac 15:13). Downers, Ill., USA: InterVarsity Press.

Acts: The Church is Born

Acts: The Church is Born

Session 8: Setting New Roots in Greece

Introduction

This week we observe Paul as he continues to carry out God's orders that he received through a vision while he was in Troas. "Come to Macedonia," the vision said. The part the vision didn't say was that the Macedonians would really not like Paul very much. Once he reached the capital city of the region – Thessalonica – his preaching caused quite a stir among the people. Many people of all social strata gave their heart to Jesus as the King. This sent the town into turmoil and instigated the great chase. A group of anti-Paul "mobsters" chased Paul out of Thessalonica and into Berea. They did not let him stay there long and forced him to flee to the coast, sail south, and hang out in Athens until Silas and Timothy were finished establishing a strong church in Berea. After sharing the resurrection of Jesus with the Greek philosophers, Paul moved on to the capital of Achaia – Corinth.

In Corinth Paul met what would become dear friends from Rome named Aquila and Priscilla. This husband and wife team became a vital aspect of Paul's life and God's Kingdom work in the world. They eventually ministered in Ephesus for a while and then returned to Rome to build the church there.

In Corinth Paul experienced a supernatural protection and was able to establish a true ministry hub among the Gentile people. Corinth was a perfect city for this operation since it was located at a crossroads of North/South trade in Greece and East/West trade across the Isthmus (a small land bridge across which sea captains would roll their ships on logs rather than cross the stormy southern coast of Greece.)

At the end of the section we are introduced to a dynamic new teacher and missionary named Apollos. This man would eventually move into Corinth and continue to build Jesus' Kingdom through his teaching ministry.

At this point of the story our tree has truly grown strong. Not only has the center shifted from Jerusalem to Antioch, but it has actually dropped seeds in Greece and begun a whole new root structure in the city of Corinth. Jesus' Kingdom was truly beginning to become a Kingdom of the world where Jews and Greeks were equal as its citizens.

Acts: The Church is Born

Session 8: Setting New Roots in Greece

Lesson 1

Acts 17:1-9

What was the heart of Paul's message in Thessalonica?

Describe Paul's following in Thessalonica, both in size and in gender/ethnic mixture.

How did the Jews respond to the following Paul built? What do you think may have been at stake for the Jews (in other words, why did they get so upset with Paul)?

What was the accusation brought against the church?

The Jewish Message – a deeper look

Thessalonica was an important city in the region of Macedonia.

> In the NT Thessalonica is referred to exclusively in connection with the apostle Paul's missionary activities (cf. Acts 17:1-13; 20:4; 27:2; 1 Thess.; 2 Thess.; Phil. 4:16; 2 Tim. 4:10). The political and religious history of the city is important for a proper understanding of these NT references. The city was founded in 316 B.C. by Cassander, a general in Alexander's army, who gave the city its name in honor of his wife, Thessalonikeia, the daughter of Philip II and the half-sister of Alexander. The new city included the ancient Therme and some thirty-five other towns. When Macedonia became a Roman province in 146 B.C., Thessalonica was made the capital and thus the center of Roman administration. The city supported the victorious Antony and Octavian prior to the battle of Philippi in 42 B.C., an event that ushered in a prosperous new era for Thessalonica. Additionally we know that the Roman statesman and orator Cicero spent part of his exile in Thessalonica in 58 B.C., that the Roman general Pompey took refuge from Julius Caesar in the city in 49 B.C., and also that such prominent literary figures as Lucian and Polyaenus visited the city. The extensive coinage of Thessalonica underscores its prosperity, certainly due to its status as a free city (i.e., one granted certain tax concessions and some other privileges) and its location as a main station on the famous Via Egnatia, which ran through the city on an east/west axis from the Balkans to Asia Minor.[1]

Today we can make two observations about Paul's ministry in this city.

First, we see a summary of his message to the Jews. Notice how Luke breaks the message down into three parts:

1. **He reasoned with them from the scriptures…**

   Once again, he spoke the language that

Acts: The Church is Born

Session 8: Setting New Roots in Greece

they understood. Paul shared a passion for the scriptures (remember, this refers to what we consider the Old Testament) and the Jews were very familiar with the process of discussing scripture on the Sabbath.

Read the following benediction. It was prayed aloud in the Synagogue every Sabbath. Can you see how easy it would be for Paul to use something like this as a launching platform for his message about Jesus?

'Blessed art Thou, the Lord our God, and the God of our fathers, the God of Abraham, the God of Isaac, and the God of Jacob: the great, the mighty and the terrible God, the most high God Who showest mercy and kindness, Who createst all things, Who rememberest the pious deeds of the patriarchs, and wilt in love bring a redeemer to their children's children for Thy Name's sake; O King, Helper, Saviour and Shield! Blessed art Thou, O Lord, the Shield of Abraham.'[2]

2. **Explaining and proving that the Christ had to suffer and rise from the dead.**

   Notice that he has not yet given away the punch line. He first speaks in the generic sense regarding the Messiah and reasons with them that the Messiah had to suffer and rise from the dead. This was contrary to the popular view of the coming Messiah. The Jews were looking for a great conqueror who would overthrow the oppressors and establish an autonomous state for Israel once again. Once a Jew was able to see that the Old Testament actually indicated that the Messiah must die and rise from the dead, then Paul was able to deal the final card.

3. **"This Jesus I am proclaiming to you is the Christ."**

   Now Paul is able to proclaim the full message of good news that Jesus of Nazareth is, indeed, the long-awaited Messiah who died and rose again to establish the Kingdom of God in the hearts of people.

The second observation is that the message of Jesus will almost always come into conflict with political power. In Thessalonica the people gathered up the rabble of the city and formed a mob to get the attention of the officials. During the 40s, the Roman Emperor had launched a series of attacks against the Jewish population of the Empire because the Jews were not willing to bow to the Emperor and worship him as a god. The Emperor had threatened the provincial rulers to not allow any of these rebellious people to form an uprising or they would pay the penalty themselves. In light of this, it is easy to see why the accusation brought against Paul would have been taken seriously.

Jesus is a serious threat to any human being who claims to have real authority – godlike authority – over the lives of other humans. The Kingdom of God with its stance for allegiance to the one true God, equality of its members, and unconditional love for all people, stands in stark contrast to the self-serving systems of the world. It will almost always come under sharp scrutiny and harsh attack.

Acts: The Church is Born

Session 8: Setting New Roots in Greece

Just For Kids

Read this Prayer out loud, together.

'Blessed are you, the Lord our God, and the God of our fathers, the God of Abraham, the God of Isaac, and the God of Jacob: the great, the mighty and the terrible God, the most high God Who shows mercy and kindness, Who creates all things, Who remembers the pious deeds of the patriarchs, and will in love bring a redeemer to their children's children for your Name's sake; O King, Helper, Savior and Shield! Blessed are you, O Lord, the Shield of Abraham.'

This is one of the prayers that the Jewish people would pray in the synagogue every Sabbath day.

When Paul went into the synagogue, which part of this prayer do you think he could use to begin teaching about Jesus?

We need to always remember that the Jews were God's chosen people for centuries before Christians came on the scene. Jesus didn't start a new religion, he just fulfilled the promise that God made to Abraham.

Spend some time praying for the Jewish people that they might see that Jesus is their Messiah.

Acts: The Church is Born

Session 8: Setting New Roots in Greece

Lesson 2

Acts 17:10-15

Why did Paul and Silas go to Berea?

Why were the Bereans "of more noble character?"

What scriptures would they have been using?

Describe the demographics of Paul's following in Berea?

Why did Paul head for Athens?

Epistle Alert!! It is most likely that somewhere within this time period Paul wrote both letters to the church in Thessalonica (1 & 2 Thessalonians). He probably wrote 1 Thessalonians from Athens and 2 Thessalonians from Corinth. If you have time, read those letters and try to see them in the context of this story.

"More Noble" Bereans

Before we dive into the Bereans, let's stop and note one important theme in this section of Acts. God used adversity to advance the mission of Paul and spread the Kingdom. In each city Paul plants a vital church, but is then driven out by adversaries. Had this not happened he may have been tempted to stay on in the first city in which he planted a good church. Thessalonica would have been an ideal spot to set up a ministry hub, since it was the capital of Macedonia and at a major cross-road of international travel. Instead, God used persecution to drive him to Berea, which was known by the Romans as "off the beaten path."

Once again, God uses strange methods that are seemingly incongruent to God's nature in order to lead and guide God's servants. Then God takes them to very unlikely places. Who would have thought that the truly "noble" people would have been in a place that was "off the beaten path?"

The Bereans were described as "more noble" than the Thessalonians. The Greek term here is "eugenesteroi" and literally means "of noble birth." However, it also has the connotation of having qualities that would normally be considered representative of those from the nobility. It is translated in different ways:

> More noble (KJV)
> More open-minded (LB)
> More noble-minded (NASB)
> More willing to listen (NCV)
> More noble character (NIV)
> More fair-minded (NKJV)
> More receptive (NRSV)

What earned them this title? It's simple. They were not gullible or naïve. They listened to Paul's message with great eagerness. They observed as he reasoned from the scripture, but they were also aware that it is possible, with the proper power of persuasion, to massage the scripture to get it to say whatever you want it to say. They didn't commit to Paul's message right away. They were polite, but they wanted to soak on it and examine the scriptures themselves to make sure that what he was saying held water and that they were not just getting caught up in the moment and being influenced by his power of persuasion.

STEVE THOMASON
following the cloud

Acts: The Church is Born

Session 8: Setting New Roots in Greece

There is a great lesson in this for all of us. We live in a world full of fast-talking salesmen who want nothing more than to "close the deal" with us. They are skilled in the art of telling us exactly what we need to hear in order to sway us to their position, without disclosing any information that might cast doubt in our mind. The last thing they want you to do is leave their presence before you buy into their pitch. This is true if you are buying a new car and if you are talking to someone about their religion. People know this is true, and as a result, the majority of people have become skeptical of the sales pitch approach to selling anything, whether it is cars or conversions.

We can learn something from this story on both sides of the equation. First, if you are listening to a teacher, be polite, listen well, and be open to what the teacher has to say, but resolve in your heart that you will check it against scripture before you jump in feet first. That means that you need to know scripture well enough to be able to discern whether a teacher is biblical or not. The challenge is to never get complacent in your study of the Bible. Always keep studying and learning the truth that God has graciously given to you so that you will be ready to test any teaching that comes your way.

On the other side of the equation, we can learn something about how to approach things when we are the one doing the teaching. Be patient with people. Don't hard-sell it. Speak the truth boldly and lovingly. Clearly present the message from scripture. Then, trust God to do God's work. Be open to questions, challenges, and criticisms. Encourage people to look into it for themselves. If you have this approach, the person you are teaching will be much more likely to want to pursue a dialogue with you if they believe that you love them as a person, are willing to give them space, and aren't just looking for another notch on your evangelistic shotgun handle. If they do the research themselves, then their faith will not be in your teaching, but in the Word of God, and they will be much more likely to have the roots of the Kingdom set in their heart for real.

Just For Kids

Get a dictionary and look up the word "noble." What did Luke mean when he said the Bereans were more noble?

What did they do that earned them this description?

Here is an important truth that everyone, grown-ups and kids alike, need to remember. There is only one teacher for the Christian; that is God. There is only one source through which God has clearly communicated to us about what we need to know; that is the Bible. As you grow up, always remember that you should never just believe what someone says simply because they are a teacher or a pastor. You need to take the time to check their teaching and see if it agrees with the Bible. That is what the Bereans did when Paul came to tell them about Jesus.

The question is whether you know your Bible well enough to know if someone is teaching the truth or making something up.

What can you do to increase your knowledge of the Bible?

Acts: The Church is Born

Session 8: Setting New Roots in Greece

Lesson 3

Acts 17:16-34

What was Paul doing in Athens?

What distress motivated Paul to begin reasoning with the people?

Where did he interact with the people of Athens when he first arrived?

Outline Paul's message to the Greek philosophers of the Aeropagus (Mars Hill). Where did he start? How did he build his case? What was the conclusion and the heart of his message?

Compare/Contrast this message to the one he preached in Pisidian Antioch in Acts 13:13-41.

How was Paul's message received?

Paul on Mars Hill

500 years before Paul visited this city, Athens was the cultural center of the world. It was here that great thinkers like Socrates, Plato, and Aristotle crafted their philosophies and changed the face of western culture forever. When Paul entered this city, it was full of beautiful architecture and an echo of its former greatness. It was still a place of learning and of exchanging ideas. Notice how Luke describes the Athenians, "[they] spent their time doing nothing but talking about and listening to the latest ideas."

While Paul did enter a Jewish synagogue in Athens, this is not the point that Luke wished to emphasize. In this city we get to see one of the greatest examples of a purely cross-cultural, evangelistic message. If we step through this message we will learn some excellent tips on how to present the good news of Jesus to people who do not have any background in scripture or the Judeo-Christian culture.

He met them where they were -- with respect. Paul complimented them on their religiousness. It's not that Paul agreed with them, but he found a common place and acknowledged their desire to know the gods and do whatever they could to please them. That's something, at least, and he praises them. How much further would he have gotten in the speech if his opening remarks were, "You dirty rotten pagan, idol worshippers. Don't you know that you are going to rot in hell for your wickedness?"

He found a common touchstone to use as a springboard. The Athenians were so concerned about pleasing the gods, and averting their wrath, that they covered all their bases by erecting an altar to the "unknown god." That was like saying, "OK, if there are any deities out there that we may have overlooked, please forgive our ignorance and don't zap us. We'd worship you too, if we knew who you were." Paul was able to use this desire to know the gods as a way to bridge the gap and open the door to discuss the idea of a different kind of god than the Athenians had ever conceived.

He used common logic and general revelation to present his case. In Romans 1 Paul expounded on this when he said that

> what may be known about God is plain to them, because God has made it plain to them. For since the creation of the world God's invisible qualities—his eternal power and divine nature—have been clearly seen, being understood from what has been made, so that men are without excuse.

Acts: The Church is Born

Session 8: Setting New Roots in Greece

For although they knew God, they neither glorified him as God nor gave thanks to him, but their thinking became futile and their foolish hearts were darkened. Although they claimed to be wise, they became fools and exchanged the glory of the immortal God for images made to look like mortal man and birds and animals and reptiles."

He used their own cultural language to emphasize the logic of his point. He didn't pull out the Bible and prove his argument with book, chapter, and verse – that would have meant nothing to these people. What he did was quote their own literature to show that their own thinkers intuitively acknowledge the truth of his proposition in the very fabric of their culture.

He didn't hold back the punch line. Many people have attacked Paul's message as "unchristian" because of its lack of scriptural reference. In the same way, many have attacked some contemporary evangelists' attempts to reach our own culture through mediums such as literature, drama, and film, as being "unchristian" because it doesn't look and smell like a church building on Sunday morning. Let's learn from Paul in that he never "watered down" the gospel at Athens. He clearly presented the truth that God created all men to worship God, and that God will not stand for people worshipping God's creation and calling it a god while they ignore the Maker. Yet, out of God's love, God has made a way for people to repent from their ignorance and be reconciled to their Creator. This way is made through the resurrection of Jesus.

Here is an important point that we can learn about the gospel message from studying Paul's ministry. The gospel is not about religion. The critique that Paul made of the Greeks was the exact same critique he made against the Jews. They exchanged the infinite, Almighty, Creator God for a set of rituals and rules and things made by human hands. The Jews clung to the Law of Moses and the Temple ritual, focusing on it instead of the God who gave it to them. The Greeks focused on the air, the wind, the water, and the creatures that God had made rather than on the God who made them. We as humans have a propensity to want to create God in our own image, mandate that God operates according to our set of standards, built an idol or a system through which to "worship" God, and then bow down to it. Paul told the Jews and the Gentiles alike that God does not desire this for God's children. God wants them to wake up from their darkness and death and step into the light of the person of Jesus. Through his resurrection he demonstrated his power over nature, sickness, and death and displayed to the world that God was knowable.

The heart of the gospel is the resurrected Jesus. That's it. Whatever cultural forms and systems you want to wrap around him is irrelevant. If the risen Lord is proclaimed, then the Kingdom of God is present. Through Him we have access to the Eternal Creator and we can call God "Abba, Father."

Acts: The Church is Born

Session 8: Setting New Roots in Greece

Just For Kids

Paul was the master of finding something in a person's culture and using it to talk about Jesus. In Athens he saw that they had an altar to an unknown god, so he started there to talk about Jesus. He also used some popular poetry that everyone knew in order to make a point. He did not use the Old Testament, because the people weren't familiar with it and it wouldn't have made any sense to them.

Spend some time talking about your own culture -- famous stories, movies, songs, historical events, etc. -- and see if there is anything that could be used as a tool to talk about Jesus, his resurrection, and salvation.

Maybe you could use these tools the next time you are talking to your friends who don't yet know Jesus.

Acts: The Church is Born

Session 8: Setting New Roots in Greece

Lesson 4

Acts 18:1-17

How did Paul spend his time when he was with Aquila and Priscilla? Where was this couple from?

What changed in Paul's daily routines when Silas and Timothy caught up with him in Corinth?

What changed in Paul's perspective toward the Jews? Why?

How was Paul's ministry received after the switch to Titius' house?

What promise did Jesus make to Paul?

How long did Paul serve in Corinth?

How did Gallio respond to the attempts to thwart Paul's ministry through legal action?

New Roots, Unlikely Place

In chapter 16 we saw that Paul was kept from going to Asia by a "divine detour." We speculated that Paul was probably intending to go to Ephesus where he could establish a nice ministry hub for the region. Instead, he was directed north to Troas, and then through a dream, was called to cross the Aegean Sea and begin planting churches in Macedonia.

Try to imagine what might have been going through Paul's mind as he made this Macedonian trip.

- In Philippi he was flogged and thrown in Jail.
- In Thessalonica he was falsely accused and run out of town by a mob.
- In Berea the Thessalonian mob chased him and ran him out of that town as well.
- He was whisked off to Athens to wait. While he was there he debated with the Greek philosophers, but received only mediocre response. Some scholars even argue that his appearance before the Aeropagus was an arrest and a trial.

"Lord, what is going on? Didn't you specifically call me to this mission? Why in the world are you making it so difficult for me? If I were in Ephesus I bet I wouldn't be having half the trouble I've had on this mission."

Perhaps Paul didn't think these things, but if we were in his shoes, it wouldn't be hard to imagine us thinking that way.

Now look what happens in Corinth. Jesus came to him in a vision and promised that no harm would come to him. Because of this divine force field placed around Paul's life in Corinth he was able to stay there for 18 months and really plant a strong church.

Corinth. Who would have thought that God had that city in mind for Paul's first Gentile ministry hub? Corinth was

> A city of Greece at the W end of the isthmus between central Greece and the Peloponnesus, in control of trade routes between N Greece and the

Acts: The Church is Born

Session 8: Setting New Roots in Greece

Peloponnese and across the isthmus. The latter was particularly important because much trade was taken across the isthmus rather than round the stormy S promontories of the Peloponnese. There were two harbours, Lechaeum 2.5 km W on the Corinthian Gulf, connected with the city by long walls; and Cenchreae 14 km E on the Saronic Gulf. Corinth thus became a flourishing centre of trade, as well as of industry, particularly ceramics. The town is dominated by the Acrocorinth (566 m), a steep, flat-topped rock surmounted by the acropolis, which in ancient times contained, *inter alia*, a temple of Aphrodite, goddess of love, whose service gave rise to the city's proverbial immorality, notorious already by the time of Aristophanes (Strabo, 378; Athenaeus, 573).[3]

Who would have thought that in this sexy, sultry, city of international trade God would choose to establish a strong mission outpost for God's Kingdom.

Be encouraged today. Your life may not have taken a path that you initially thought it would take. You may have even gone through some very difficult trials along the way. But, it is possible for God to do great and miraculous things in the most unlikely places. Our job is to keep our eyes and our hearts fixed on God, listen to God's instruction, and simply obey. If God tells you to let yourself get beat up as you travel through Macedonia, then keep going. If God tells you to set up a tent shop in Corinth, then settle down and do it. It's God's Kingdom and we are simply following orders.

Just For Kids

Have you ever made a tent out of blankets and chairs? Paul was a tent-maker. In our story today, it says that while Paul was waiting for his friends, Silas and Timothy, to arrive, he made tents with two new friends, a husband and wife team, named Aquila and Priscilla.

Have some fun right now and make a tent out of some blankets and some chairs. Pretend that you are Paul, Aquila, and Priscilla.

Now, have one person pretend to be Paul and get inside the tent.

Have everyone else pretend to be Paul's adversaries. Each person should take a piece of paper, wad it up, and pretend it is a stone or an evil accusation that is ready to be thrown at Paul.

Have someone read Jesus' words,

"Do not be afraid; keep on speaking, do not be silent. For I am with you, and no one is going to attack and harm you, because I have many people in this city.

Have all the bad guys throw their paper toward the tent. Did Paul get hit?

The lesson for today is that, when God has called you to a ministry God will protect you. No matter what people say against you, God will protect you.

Acts: The Church is Born

Session 8: Setting New Roots in Greece

Lesson 5

Acts 18:18-28

Where was Paul heading? What is in that region?

Why did Paul have his hair cut off?

Describe Apollos.

In what way did Aquila and Priscilla help Apollos?

In what way did Apollos' ministry overlap and intersect with Paul's? Where?

Paul Returns to Antioch

Here are two observations from today's reading.

Paul took the spiritual disciplines seriously. When he had his hair cut off it is most likely that he had just completed the process of a Nazarite vow.

> NAZIRITE (Heb. nazi'r, from nazar, 'to separate, consecrate, abstain'; cf. nezer, 'a diadem', the 'crown of God', sometimes identified with the Nazirite's uncut hair). In Israel the Nazirite was one who separated himself from others by consecration to Yahweh with a special vow.
>
> The origin of the practice is pre-Mosaic and obscure. Semites and other primitive peoples often left the hair uncut during some undertaking calling for divine help, and thereafter consecrated the hair (cf. modern echoes of this among Arab tribes in A. Lods, Israel, 1932, p. 305; see also Jdg. 5:2).[4]

If you would like to learn more about the Nazarite Vow, read Numbers 6.

Many people have said that Paul moved completely away from his Jewish heritage and started a new religion called Christianity. That is not true. Paul did not despise his heritage, nor did he deny the beneficial aspects of the Law that God gave to God's people. It's not that Paul walked away from his religion; he stepped above it to see a broader perspective.

We can learn something from this. Within the Old Testament there is a wealth of practical wisdom that will lead to life and health. The dietary laws were given for protection. The model of the Tabernacle gives us a wonderful visual image of how to approach God in worship. The civil laws give us good guidelines for how to get along with one another. We do not have to follow these laws in order to earn God's favor, but these laws are still valid and evidence that God has always cared and provided for God's people in every aspect of life. We don't know why, but we do know that Paul took up the spiritual discipline of the Nazarite. This was a type of fast – from fermented drink and other such things – for a period of time in order to hear more clearly from God and/or fulfill a mission. Paul, even in his state of radical grace, saw the value in tapping into a very ancient spiritual discipline to help him grow deeper in

Acts: The Church is Born

Session 8: Setting New Roots in Greece

his relationship with God.

Ask God to show you some disciplines that might help you cultivate your walk with him.

Paul wasn't the only kid on the block. Apollos enters the picture. While he doesn't get much ink in the book of Acts, Apollos was a major player in the early church. The fact that Luke includes him in the story is evidence of his significant role. One of the reasons that Paul may have included Apollos was to show the connection between Paul and Apollos. While Paul never directly mentored Apollos, Aquila and Priscilla did.

Up to this point in time Apollos had only known the message of Jesus through he lenses of John's baptism. It is likely that Apollos heard the message of John's Jewish rite of water baptism of repentance and then of Jesus' resurrection, but not of the events of Pentecost. Perhaps Apollos himself had been in Jerusalem prior to Pentecost and heard of Jesus, or a traveler had informed him. Regardless of how it happened, somehow Apollos had an accurate, but incomplete picture of Jesus. It is interesting that Luke does not tell us exactly what was deficient in Apollos' teaching or what Aquila and Priscilla's "more adequate" understanding was specifically. Based upon the mentioning of the fact that Apollos only knew of John's baptism, it is probable that Apollos was not aware of the outpouring of the Holy Spirit and the power of the Spirit along with the power of the Word. He had the Word part down, but perhaps lacked the power of the Spirit. Yet, on the other hand, since this was such a strong theme for Luke, it is curious as to why Luke would not have highlighted this point in Apollos' ministry.

If you read Paul's letters to the Corinthians you will discover that after Apollos went to Corinth and preached the gospel there, the church began to divide into factions. Some followed Paul, some followed Apollos, some followed Peter, etc. (1 Corinthians 1:10-17) It is most likely that Luke included this story of Apollos, Aquila, and Priscilla to demonstrate that there was unity between Paul and Apollos and the divisions being created in the church based upon the teaching and theological nuances of different teachers was ludicrous. As Paul wrote in Ephesians, "Make every effort to keep the unity of the Spirit through the bond of peace. 4 There is one body and one Spirit— just as you were called to one hope when you were called— 5 one Lord, one faith, one baptism; 6 one God and Father of all, who is over all and through all and in all. (Ephesians 4:3-6)

Just For Kids

Let's end our week of study by mapping out chapter 17 and 18.

Find these key cities on your map

- Thessalonica
- Berea
- Athens
- Corinth
- Ephesus
- Caesarea
- Syria
- Galatia
- Phrygia
- Alexandria

(Footnotes)

[1] Achtemeier, P. J., Harper & Row, P., & Society of Biblical Literature. (1985). *Harper's Bible dictionary*. Includes index. (1st ed.) (Page 1065). San Francisco: Harper & Row.

[2] Wood, D. R. W. (1996). New Bible dictionary (3rd ed. /) (Page 1143). Leicester, England; Downers Grove, Ill.: InterVarsity Press.

[3] Wood, D. R. W., & Marshall, I. H. (1996). *New Bible dictionary* (3rd ed. /) (Pages 223-224). Leicester, England; Downers Grove, Ill.: InterVarsity Press.

[4] Wood, D. R. W. (1996). New Bible dictionary (3rd ed. /) (Page 808). Leicester, England; Downers Grove, Ill.: InterVarsity Press.

Acts: The Church is Born

Acts: The Church is Born

Session 9: Finishing in Greece

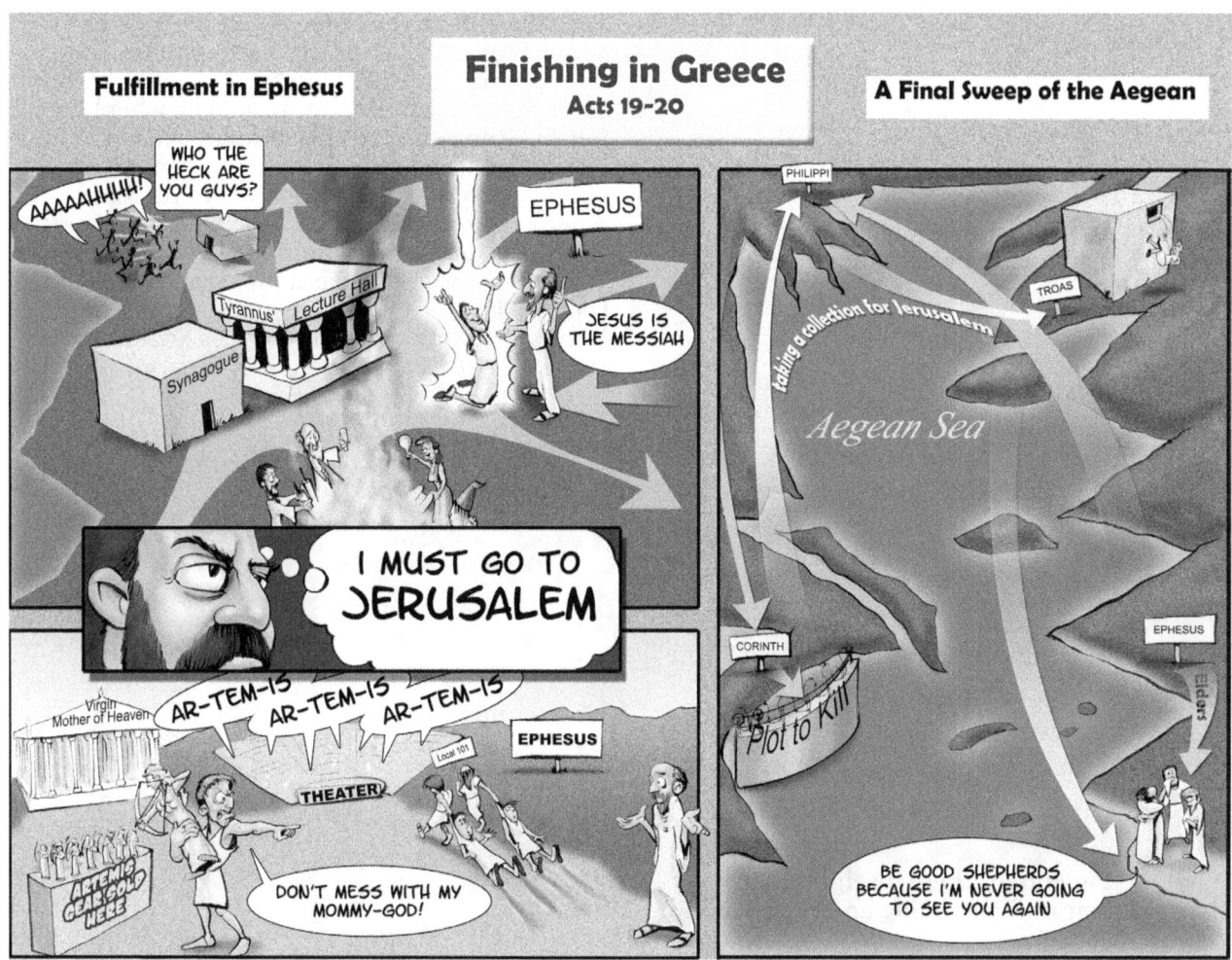

Introduction

This week we conclude Paul's missionary journeys. After a quick visit back to Antioch and a tour through the first churches in Galatia, Paul finally realizes his dream and sets up a base of operation in Ephesus. From this centralized city Paul was able to spend between two and three years demonstrating God's power, teaching and instructing disciples in the Way, and planting churches through his disciples in all the cities in the outlying region.

After his work was done in Ephesus, Paul set his eyes on Jerusalem and determined to collect a financial offering from all the churches in the region in order to bring aid to the famine-stricken Jerusalem. Paul traveled through Macedonia and Achaia, visiting his churches and taking up the collection. He intended to sail directly from Corinth to Caesarea, but a plot to kill him forced him to turn around and retrace his steps through Macedonia. After stopping in Troas and the coast off of Ephesus, Paul and his multicultural traveling party set sail for Caesarea.

In this section we will see Paul experience the extremes of ministry. At one point he is experiencing great heights of power and glory as the Holy Spirit heals people and teaches people through him. Then, in the same city a riot rises up against him and he has to leave. Such is the way of ministry. We can learn a great deal through the roller coaster ride that Paul endured and observe how he maintained focus through it all.

Acts: The Church is Born

Session 9: Finishing in Greece

Lesson 1

Acts 19:1-20

Where is Apollos ministering at this time? What connections did Paul have to that place?

What kind of baptism did the disciples have?

What was their understanding of the Holy Spirit?

What did Paul do for these disciples that changed their understanding and experience of being a disciple?

Compare this event with other conversion accounts in Acts.

2:4; 8:15–17; 9:17, 18; 10:44; 13:48, 52; 16:31–34; 18:8; 19:6

Read the following commentary on this event. Do you agree? Why or why not?

Whatever we may believe about the 'normal' conversion, Luke seems to have emphasized mention of these gifts and the reception of the Holy Spirit in his account primarily where he felt that the church or his readers needed to be assured that the group to which the converts belonged were really acceptable to the Lord, *e.g.* the Samaritans (ch. 8), the Gentiles (ch. 10) and these disciples of John. As mentioned in the Commentary on those other passages, the way that Luke records these events suggests that for him they functioned as much as a sign to the missionaries as to the converts themselves.[1]

Where was the base of Paul's extended ministry in Ephesus? Why?

Geographically, what kind of impact did Paul's ministry have in this place?

What miraculous events happened as the result of Paul's ministry in Ephesus?

Why were the sons of Sceva not able to get rid of the evil spirits?

What impact did the power of Jesus' name have on the city of Ephesus? (vv. 17-20)

Acts: The Church is Born

Session 9: Finishing in Greece

A Realized Dream

It finally happened. The events of Acts 19:1-20 are the ministry that Paul had probably envisioned from the beginning. Remember in chapter 16 that Paul was initially kept from entering the region of Asia. Instead, God led him through Macedonia, Achaia, and eventually into Corinth. He spent 18 months in Corinth, and then passed by Ephesus as he reconnected to the church in Syrian Antioch first and then revisited the Galatian churches in order to strengthen and encourage them. Now, after that entire divine detour, Paul has come to Ephesus. This was the city that really made sense for doing ministry. It was the hub of Asia. From this port city the entire region could be evangelized.

Here is one important lesson from this section: It's not that God does not want to give us our desires, it's just that sometimes we get the timing mixed up. It's as if God said, "Right idea, wrong timing." Ephesus was not ready for Paul, or Paul was not ready for Ephesus. In either case, God knew exactly what God was doing.

If you have a dream, don't give up on it if it doesn't work out right away. As with everything, simply hold on to it loosely, submit to the leadership of the Holy Spirit, be faithful where God plants you, and be patient. If it is a desire that God has given to you, then it will eventually work out, in God's timing.

The Power of the Name

When we think of evangelism we typically think of working with an individual, or perhaps a family. In today's reading we are exposed to a bigger picture. When Paul went into a place, he looked at an entire region. Ephesus wasn't just a little town; it was the epicenter of a huge region of the Empire and it would require an all-out artillery assault to establish the Kingdom of God in this region.

Before we dive into Paul's story, let's look honestly at a subject that many Evangelicals don't really like to acknowledge. The fact is that, many times, before a missionary can begin reaching people life by life, there needs to be some spiritual warfare at the regional level. Satan's power has control over whole cities and regions. This is evident in the story of Jesus' temptation. When Satan tempted Jesus he offered to give Jesus all the Kingdoms of the world if Jesus would only bow down to him. Did satan have the authority to make that offer? Apparently he did because Jesus did not question him. Jesus simply said, "Away from me, Satan! For it is written, 'Worship the Lord your God, and serve him only.'" Paul later wrote to the church that he would eventually plant in Ephesus and reminded them that their struggle was not against flesh and blood but against the rulers, against the authorities, against the powers of this dark world and against the spiritual forces of evil in the heavenly realms.

For millennium human beings have willingly surrendered control of their lives over to satan's authority and have allowed him to blind them to the truth of God's love for them. Each region has been duped by a different deception. Some believe that they are under the tyrannical authority of heartless gods who demand sacrifice and care nothing for human beings. Others live in fear of the evil spirits that lurk in the forest. Still others believe that the earth is a benign energy field that can be manipulated by secret knowledge and harnessed for the will of the one who understands the incantation. While others live, perhaps most insidiously, in the belief that there is no such thing as the supernatural at all and that humanity is nothing more than a highly evolved animal that operates on the philosophy of "survival of the fittest." Whatever the deception may be, it is a reality that has a powerful grip on the hearts of all the people in that region, and it is a stronghold that can only be brought down by the power of the name of Jesus and the fervent prayer of his people.

Let's observe how this plays out in Ephesus:

Ephesus was no ordinary region. God had to pull out the big guns for this mission. Paul's first encounter with the "disciples" helps us understand the fact that Ephesus was a mixed up place. Paul met twelve men who appeared to be disciples, yet they didn't even know about Jesus. All they knew was the ministry of John the Baptist which was a purely Jewish rite of repentance. Their knowledge was incomplete. They had not heard the message of the Messiah, they had only heard the message of repentance in preparation for the Messiah. That's like hearing a joke without getting the punchline, or dressing up for the dance and never leaving the house. When Paul explained the message of Jesus, then they got to laugh and dance. They were ready to be baptized into the name of Jesus, cross over from the Old Testament, and receive the Holy Spirit. When Paul laid his hands on them the Holy Spirit showed up in a big way. As with every other huge gap-bridging experience in Acts so far, when the Holy Spirit first came to a region, it showed up as a mini day of Pentecost. This was the earmark that said, "OK everyone, an official apostle of Jesus is on the scene, the teaching you are about to

Acts: The Church is Born

Session 9: Finishing in Greece

receive is authentic, and the believers who come to Jesus under this ministry will be in unity with the church in Jerusalem, Samaria, and all the regions heretofore evangelized." It's like when an explorer reaches a new territory and plants his flag down in previously uncharted land and declares this place for his kingdom. The Holy Spirit had now come to Ephesus. It's showtime!

Normally, Paul would move into a city and begin by reasoning from the scripture with the Jews in the synagogue to convince them that Jesus was the long-awaited Messiah. From this core of believers, who were well-versed in scripture, Paul could then branch out to the Greeks and build the church. In Ephesus things were different. Ephesus was a town that was steeped in pagan religion, witchcraft, sorcery, and religious syncretism (the blending of many religions into one). It seems that even the Jews in Ephesus were steeped in a syncretistic religion in which they mixed the Law of Moses with the witchcraft and sorcery of the Ephesians. We've seen this before in the lives of Simon the Magician in Samaria and Elymas the Sorcerer on Cyprus. Here the whole city was blinded. So much so that Paul gave up trying to convince them and acknowledged that his ministry in Ephesus was a completely "Jesus vs. Pagan" encounter.

From here we can point out three important aspects of Paul's ministry in Ephesus that will help us understand what it takes to reach a region.

Paul had a ministry of healing. Paul's healing ministry was beyond that of the simple loving touch of a kind person. It was dramatic and powerful. Luke even says that it was extraordinary. It was so extraordinary that even handkerchiefs that had touched him brought healing to people. This is very parallel to the story of the woman who touched the hem of Jesus' robe and was healed. Sometimes the grip on a region is so strong that God has to bring out the big guns to pull down the stronghold. This healing demonstrated a power that was beyond the scope of one man and demonstrated the power of Jesus to the region. When a region is so steeped in darkness, the first thing it needs is healing and deliverance.

It wasn't magical power. The region was so steeped in magic that the Jewish sorcerers thought that Paul was simply bringing another magical incantation into the mix. The seven sons of Sceva were used to driving out the evil spirits through their syncretized Jewish/Pagan magic. Then one day they tried to use their new incantation – the name of Jesus – and they were faced with a stark reality. You see, up to this point the evil spirits were playing with them and allowing the "exorcists" to drive them out with their magic in order to convince them that they did have power through their incantations. Now, however, when the one truth in the universe was presented, the demons reacted accordingly. Here is the really important piece of this; *the healing that comes from God isn't magic*. The name of Jesus isn't a trick or an incantation. The reason the Sceva boys got their magical tails whipped was because they did not have a relationship with the Jesus they were claiming. The power of Jesus comes through a surrendered heart that is in an authentic relationship with him, not a powerful person who wields his name. Just like Peter told Simon the Magician, you cannot purchase or coerce the power of God. You can simply be the surrendered conduit of it. It's not about the human healer; it's about the risen King.

The power got their attention. Notice what happened after the Sceva boys ran into the truth about the spiritual battle and the name of Jesus. The power struck fear in the region. People's eyes were opened for the first time. They openly confessed their sins. They repented of their sins to the point of burning a fortune's worth of witchcraft paraphernalia. At that point the stronghold over Ephesus was broken and the word of Jesus spread quickly and grew in power.

In 21st century America we live in a pluralistic culture where syncretism is the rule of the day. For the past 150 years, naturalism has dominated our religious landscape, so much so that nearly every school child is convinced, from the time they are in pre-school, that they are nothing more than apes. In the last 30-40 years the bankruptcy of modernism and naturalism has created a spiritual hunger in our nation and has driven millions of people to the spirituality of pantheism, the New Age, and spiritists. Calling your psychic hotline, having a fortune teller at your company party, and reading your horoscope have become commonplace. The scary thing is that this naturalistic/pantheistic worldview is so pervasive that it has seeped its way deeply into the Christian community. In many ways we are like the city of Ephesus and our churches are the like its synagogues.

What will reach the cities of America in the 21st century? Nothing will reach them short of the power of God demonstrated in the lives of God's people. We have been sent in the name of Jesus, under his authority, to break these strongholds and to bring the healing power of the Kingdom

Acts: The Church is Born

Session 9: Finishing in Greece

of God to God's people. How do we do that? The first step is to acknowledge the reality of the spiritual battle. Second, is to be sure that the armor of God is firmly placed in our lives each day. That means that we need to bask in the truth that God has set us free (breastplate of righteousness), trust that Jesus holds it all together (belt of truth), know that we are at peace with God and stand on solid ground (feet fitted with good news of peace), daily reconnect to our relationship with Jesus (helmet of salvation), daily study and proclaim the word of God (sword of the spirit), believe that all of the above is actually true (shield of faith) Third, and finally, pray continually for the deliverance and salvation of people.

Paul did not go into Ephesus with a big show or a self-promoting power trip. He simply went in, having the armor firmly in place, and allowed himself to be an open conduit of the Holy Spirit. He taught daily in the lecture hall, he healed people, and he trusted that God would do God's work through him if he would simply stay out of the way. Imagine what would happen if the churches in our valley united in this way and prayed to break the strongholds that grip our city. Imagine what would happen if the people in our own community experienced the transforming power and healing touch of Jesus in their hearts and relationships. The Kingdom of God would become an unstoppable force.

Just for Kids

What did the magicians do when they gave their life to Jesus? What did they burn? Why?

Sometimes in life there are things that get in the way of our ability to love God with our whole heart. Do you have anything like that?

Write the things down on a piece of paper that are bad attitudesor habits that get in your way and keep you from experiencing and demonstrating God's love. Maybe things like anger, bitterness, fear, addiction, etc.

If you have a grill, take those pieces of paper and, under the supervision of your parents, of course, burn those things.

We need to be willing to throw anything into the fire that is causing us to sin and be apart from God's love. Are you willing to do that?

Acts: The Church is Born

Session 9: Finishing in Greece

Lesson 2

Acts 19:21-22

Read Luke 9:51-53. What parallel do you see between today's reading and this passage?

Read Romans 15:24-28. Why was Paul heading to Jerusalem, and why was he passing through Greece to get there?

Who did Paul send on through Macedonia ahead of him?

**Epistle Alert!!! It is most likely that the Epistles of 1 & 2 Corinthians were written at this time.

Paul sets His Heart toward Jerusalem

At this point you may be wondering why we wasted a whole day's worth of reading on two measly verses. That's a fair question.

Sometimes it is important to stop and notice the little things. Sometimes it is the little things that go unnoticed but make all the difference in the world.

The point of setting aside today's reading is to highlight the fact that Luke, as the author of Luke/Acts, is drawing a definite parallel between the life of Jesus and the life of Paul.

Here is a quick outline of Jesus' life according to Luke:

> Early ministry where he experienced great victory and power. During this time he only ministered in Galilee and never went to Jerusalem (Luke 1-8)

> Jesus' Galilean ministry comes to a climax of great power that leads Peter to proclaim that he is the Christ, and then he is transfigured before their eyes. (ch. 9)

> In 9:51 Jesus "resolutely set out for Jerusalem."

> From this point on in the story Jesus' ministry turns tough as he marches toward Jerusalem where he is arrested and handed over to the Romans to be killed. (Luke 10-24)

Look at Paul's life:

> He spends the first part of his ministry in the Gentile regions (his Galilee).

> His ministry reaches its climax with a dramatic display of God's power in Ephesus.

> In 19:21 Paul decided to go to Jerusalem. From this point on he becomes single-minded and later says that he is "bound by the Spirit to go to Jerusalem."

Acts: The Church is Born

Session 9: Finishing in Greece

For the rest of his story Paul goes to Jerusalem, is accused by the Jewish leaders, is handed over to the Romans, and taken prisoner to Rome.

There is a reason that Luke highlights these parallels between Jesus and Paul. Paul was constantly attacked and accused of not being a legitimate apostle because he was not one of the original twelve. Many of his enemies tried to use the fact that his calling came later (if at all) to undermine his teaching in every city. Paul's heart was wrenched by these opponents. As his disciple and friend, one of Luke's main agendas for the book of Acts was to demonstrate that Paul was, indeed, an authentic apostle, who had been called directly by the risen Jesus, and had even paralleled Jesus' ministry in his own. It is important for us to realize and believe this since a vast majority of the New Testament flows from the mind of Paul and his theology.

The Corinthian Letters

It would be too much to ask you to read 1 and 2 Corinthians right now, but if you had time it would be a wonderful experience. It is important to remember that the majority of Paul's letters were written in the context of his life in the book of Acts. At this point in the story, in today's reading, Paul had previously spent eighteen months planting a church in Corinth and then had left for Antioch in Syria (his home base, remember). While he was in Antioch, Aquila and Priscilla were instructing Apollos in the full gospel of Jesus. As Paul traveled back through Galatia and headed for Ephesus, Apollos sailed across the Aegean to Corinth where he picked up on Paul's ministry and advanced the Kingdom even further.

Trade and travel between Ephesus and Corinth was common since they were both major international ports and were directly across the Aegean Sea from each other, so, when Paul arrived in Ephesus he received word from Corinth that things were not going well. Sin was running rampant in the Corinthian church and this troubled Paul greatly. Being the concerned spiritual father that he was, not to mention the fact that he may have had a strong and heated personality at times, Paul wrote a scathing letter to the Corinthians.

This harsh letter was his first letter, but it was not 1 Corinthians. Confused? Most people don't realize that the letters we call 1 & 2 Corinthians are actually letters 2 and 4. 1 Corinthians indicates that Paul had already written to them and that the first letter was harsh. He must have received a response and a report from his courier that the Corinthians felt a bit pistol-whipped by that letter, so in the second letter (our 1 Corinthians) he apologizes for his harshness, and restates his admonition of the church in different, yet very strong terms. Apparently this letter did the trick and evoked repentance from the people. Paul sent a third letter to congratulate them, but we do not have that letter (we know of it because it is referenced in 2 Corinthians). After Paul left Ephesus he set out for Corinth by way of Macedonia. On his way he sent the fourth letter (our 2 Corinthians). Apparently, after the discipline and repentance that came through the first three letters, some people began to question whether Paul was a legitimate apostle and spread seeds of doubt in the church. The Corinthian church became divided into factions according to loyalties to different teachers. Some people latched on to Apollos and really liked him better than Paul. Others felt that the Apollos lovers were betraying their founding father, Paul. So, Paul wrote this letter to squelch that kind of thinking and nip it in the bud.

The second reason for the fourth letter was to prepare the people for the collection that Paul was going to take from them for the church in Jerusalem. This information really helps us understand this section of Acts. During this time, the city of Jerusalem had come into hard times. There was a famine and the people were suffering. Worst of all was the fact that Christians were suffering. Paul felt compelled to travel through Macedonia and Greece to take up a collection from the "Gentile churches" and bring relief for their brothers and sisters who were suffering in Jerusalem. That is why he felt compelled to go to Jerusalem, even though he knew that it would only bring him hardship. It was important for him to demonstrate the unity of the global body of Christ in a time of need.

So, you see, there were only two verses in the reading, but in-between the lines there was a lot of important stuff.

Acts: The Church is Born

Session 9: Finishing in Greece

Just for Kids

Read Romans 15:24-28.

Why did Paul want to go to Jerusalem?

Think back to the earlier part of Paul's story. Did the people in Jerusalem really like Paul that much? Many of them really didn't like him. Isn't it amazing that Paul was willing to do something nice for a group of people that weren't that nice to him in the past?

Think of someone that may have been mean to you. If you knew they were poor and hungry now, would you be willing to bring them food and money?

Acts: The Church is Born

Session 9: Finishing in Greece

Lesson 3

Acts 19:23-41

What was at stake for Demetrius? Why was he angry at Paul?

Read the following articles on Artemis:

> **ARTEMIS**. This was the Greek name of the goddess identified with the Latin Diana of classical mythology. The name Artemis is pre-Greek. She first appears in Greek literature as mistress and protectress of wild life. (*Cf.* W. K. C. Guthrie, *The Greeks and their Gods*, 1950, pp. 99ff.) In Greece proper she was worshipped as the daughter of Zeus and Leto, and twin sister of Apollo. Horror at the pains her mother endured at her birth is supposed to have made her averse to marriage. She was goddess of the moon and of hunting, and is generally portrayed as a huntress, wild dogs in attendance. Her temple at *Ephesus was one of the seven wonders of the world, and here worship of the 'virgin goddess' appears to have been fused with some kind of fertility-cult of the mother-goddess of Asia Minor. The temple was supported on 100 massive columns, some of which were sculptured. Tradition claims that her image fell there from the sky (Acts 19:35), and is thought to refer to a meteorite; Pliny tells of a huge stone above the entrance, said to have been placed there by Diana herself. Her worship was conducted by eunuch priests, called *megabyzoi* (Strabo, 14. 1. 23), and archaeologists have discovered statues depicting her with many breasts. The silversmiths who made small votary shrines, portraying the goddess in a recess with her lions in attendance, or possibly souvenir models of the temple, caused the riot when Paul was ministering there (Acts 19:23–20:1). Their cry of 'Great is Artemis of the Ephesians!' (Acts 19:28, 34) is attested by inscriptions from Ephesus which call her 'Artemis the Great' (*CIG*, 2963c; *Greek Inscriptions in the British Museum*, iii, 1890, 481. 324).[2]

> As often, religious piety becomes a thin cloak for personal economic interests. The temple of Artemis served as a bank as well as a temple, and people from all over the world deposited funds there. About A.D. 44 (roughly a decade before Paul's arrival), inscriptions there show that the proconsul had to get involved in the temple treasury due to some serious financial irregularities: temple monies were being funneled to private individuals. In Ephesus, politics and religion were as heavily intertwined as religion and economics, and local civic pride was inseparable from the worship of the Ephesian Artemis.[3]

Describe the nature of the crowd that assembled in the theater.

Why did Paul not stand to defend himself or his partners?

Why did the crowd not listen to Alexander?

What finally motivated the crowd to disband?

Acts: The Church is Born

Session 9: Finishing in Greece

Who's Your Mommy?

As you read this passage it may be tempting to think that there are no relevant parallels to our lives and skip right over it. After all, there aren't any temples to a goddess in our city, right? Don't be too sure about that. Let's explore what was going on in Ephesus before we completely shut it out. You may find more than you bargained for.

In many pagan cultures, they believed that there was a male god and a female god and that through the copulation of these gods, life was perpetuated. By worshipping these gods, the people would insure that the crops would come in and that the cycle of life would be perpetuated. Within the gods themselves there was a constant struggle for power between the male and female and the struggle was filled with treachery and deceit.

Ephesus was dominated by a goddess figure. Artemis (also known as Diana) was considered to be the Virgin Mother of Heaven. She was a symbol of fertility. Throughout the Old Testament the people of God battled against the fertility goddess of various cultures. In each of these cultures there is a consistent theme of a dominant female figure that does not need the control or influence of a male.

In Judaism, Yahweh was always presented in a masculine form. He was the Father. At first glance it would appear that Judaism (and subsequently, Christianity) was simply the conflict between a masculine dominated culture versus a feminine dominated culture. This is not the case, however. Here's the thing. Yahweh, the Great I AM, Creator of all things is not a male or a female. In Genesis 1, it says that God created man in His image, male and female he created them. Did you catch that? Male and Female. God's image is reflected when male and female live in harmonious interdependence with one another. God's design for the male/female relationship is for them to live in mutual submission to one another as they come under the authority of God. At the fall, Adam and Eve became separated from God and became separated from each other. Eve sought after man's authority, and man sought after the toil of the earth. Thus, the battle of the sexes began.

So, if God is not a man or a woman, then why is God always referred to as "Father" or "He" in the Bible? In order to understand why God was presented as masculine, we need to look at the natural developmental process of a human child. A newborn has a very special relationship with its mother. The child emerges from the mother's body. The child feeds off of the mother's body directly. There is a very organic and physical connection between the two. The Father, on the other hand, has a very different relationship with the child. He contributes his part of the equation long before there is even knowledge of a coming child. In unhealthy scenarios, the father is often absent and, at best, the father is detached from the life of the child in a fundamental way because he cannot produce the food it needs to survive. For this reason, young children tend to bond more with the mother than the father. In healthy development, a child must go through a rite of passage in which they transition from a co-dependency on the mother to a place where they see the father as a vital role in the family; as the one who is the leader and provider for the family. Since this relationship is not as organic as that with the mother, it requires a cognitive step of faith and a moving away from the mother into a rational relationship with the father. If the child does not make this transition then it will most likely stay in a very enmeshed and co-dependent state with its "Mommy" into adulthood, thus squelching the child's ability to mature. In the transition to the father, the child learns independence and what it means to live in an interdependent state within the family unit.

The children of Israel were like God's child. While they were in slavery in Egypt they had been heavily influenced by the god/goddess myths of the Egyptian religion. Because of the power struggle between men and women, most of the ancient cultures felt more connected to the earth and the feminine spirit of the earth, thinking that the female energy is what created their food and sustenance, so they worshipped "Mother Earth." It was the male energy that brought thunder and lightning and pain and anger and wrath on the earth. Who would want to worship that? In other words, those pagan cultures never grew up and so they became enmeshed with the feminine spirit of the earth. God presented God's self to Israel in a masculine form in order to bring balance to this trend and to "wean" God's people off of the milk-suckling immaturity that comes from worshipping the earth. They needed to understand that God was not the earth and that God was transcendent (above and beyond) the earth. God was not transcendent like the sun (RA) or the thunder and lighting (Zeus). God was transcendent beyond all created things and even beyond the idea of male and female itself. God's masculine identity had to be presented to bring God's children out of darkness. Only then could God's people understand the interdependent nature of

114

Acts: The Church is Born

Session 9: Finishing in Greece

humanity's relationship between a transcendent God, each other, and the world in which we were placed.

Here's the caution for us. A great deal of "Virgin Mother of Heaven" thinking has crept into the church. The obvious place this has happened is in the non-biblical exaltation of Mary. It is a simple fact that the Mary cult evolved in the Roman Church because of what we have been discussing. The people of the Empire were used to having a female god figure. Many of the early Christians took the masculine imagery of the Old Testament and distorted it to be a license to oppress women and keep them in slavery to men. This male-dominated form of Christianity simply perpetuated the age-old struggle between men and women and caused the people to search for a feminine counterpart in the apparently male-dominated Godhead. The people reasoned, "if there is only a Father, then how in the world could the earth have been created? Don't you need a mother, too?" So, they looked at Mary as the mother of God, and exalted her to the place of the Christian goddess. This is very dangerous and has kept a lot of well intentioned people in a state of blindness in which they have not been able to see the fullness of God clearly.

Before we Protestants get all smug about this, let's understand that there is a "Virgin Mother of Heaven" problem in the Protestant side of the equation as well. In some ways it may be even more dangerous. Have you ever noticed that the stereotypical Christian organization has a feminine domination? Some have said that the church has become "sissified". Women tend to dominate while men are emasculated and powerless. Just look at how men are portrayed on television. Men are either overbearing jerks, or they are stupid, bumbling apes who don't have a shred of common sense and behave like children or animals. It's the woman who is in touch with her feelings and has a level head about things. Do you think this caricature that is portrayed through the media is an accident?

This distortion of gender roles has its grip on the church. This is evident in the fact that one of the most controversial verses in the Bible for the church today is Ephesians 5:22, "wives submit to your husbands." "That's un-American," we liberated Americans decry, "That's not Christian! God would never ask a woman to subject herself to an overbearing, male-chauvinist pig (after all, that's what men are, aren't they?)!"

Somehow, Christian men in America have become intimidated by this message and have handed over the Spiritual authority in the home and in the church to the women. God's desire for God's people, as it has been since the day God created us in God's image, was for the male and female to live in an interdependent relationship that submits to the authority of God. We don't want a masculine dominated church. We don't want a feminine dominated church. We want a God dominated church where men understand their place of servant leadership in their home as the leader and provider, and women understand their role as partner and nurturer.

Once again we can see that this was a big issue in Ephesus because it is from the letter that he wrote to this church where we see this principle most strongly taught. In Ephesians Paul talks about unity in the church, and then calls for mutual submission in the marriage relationship. Read Ephesians 5:15-33.

You know Paul was stepping on toes with the message of the Kingdom of God because the Artemis followers came after him with a vengeance. We are not sure exactly what happened, but other places in Acts and the tone of Paul's letters after his time in Ephesus indicate that Paul was deeply marked in Ephesus because of the persecution he suffered there. Here's the message for us: Any time you preach God's truth that rubs against the main flow of society – even within the church – you will almost always experience harsh resistance. Take heart. This world is not our home. We must live for the Kingdom of God at all costs.

Acts: The Church is Born

Session 9: Finishing in Greece

Just for Kids

Who was Artemis?

Read this article to learn more about her.

> ARTEMIS. This was the Greek name of the goddess identified with the Latin Diana of classical mythology. The name Artemis is pre-Greek. She first appears in Greek literature as mistress and protectress of wild life. (*Cf.* W. K. C. Guthrie, *The Greeks and their Gods*, 1950, pp. 99ff.) In Greece proper she was worshipped as the daughter of Zeus and Leto, and twin sister of Apollo. Horror at the pains her mother endured at her birth is supposed to have made her averse to marriage. She was goddess of the moon and of hunting, and is generally portrayed as a huntress, wild dogs in attendance. Her temple at *EPHESUS was one of the seven wonders of the world, and here worship of the 'virgin goddess' appears to have been fused with some kind of fertility-cult of the mother-goddess of Asia Minor. The temple was supported on 100 massive columns, some of which were sculptured. Tradition claims that her image fell there from the sky (Acts 19:35), and is thought to refer to a meteorite; Pliny tells of a huge stone above the entrance, said to have been placed there by Diana herself. Her worship was conducted by eunuch priests, called *megabyzoi* (Strabo, 14. 1. 23), and archaeologists have discovered statues depicting her with many breasts. The silversmiths who made small votary shrines, portraying the goddess in a recess with her lions in attendance, or possibly souvenir models of the temple, caused the riot when Paul was ministering there (Acts 19:23–20:1). Their cry of 'Great is Artemis of the Ephesians!' (Acts 19:28, 34) is attested by inscriptions from Ephesus which call her 'Artemis the Great' (*CIG*, 2963c; *Greek Inscriptions in the British Museum*, iii, 1890, 481. 324).[4]

The problem with the Ephesians is that they wanted to have only a female god, not the one true God.

Describe what a Mom is supposed to be like.

Describe what a Dad is supposed to be like.

One of the mistakes people make is to think that one of these is more important than the other. Some people think Dads should rule the house like a slave master and tell everyone what to do by barking orders and being tough. Others think that Moms should run the house and make the decisions while the Dad just goes off to work and comes home to watch TV. Neither one of these ideas is what God wants. God wants men and women, husbands and wives, to work together and use their differences to be a strong team that is under the leadership of God.

Is that what your family is like? Why or why not?

Acts: The Church is Born

Session 9: Finishing in Greece

Lesson 4

Acts 20:1-12

What cities did Paul visit? What is the obvious reason for choosing these cities?

How long did Paul stay in Greece (most likely in Corinth)?

**Epistle Alert!! It is most likely that it was at this time, from the city of Corinth, that Paul wrote the letter to the Romans.

Read Romans 16. Do any of these names sound familiar after having read Acts so far?

What do we know happened to Aquila and Priscilla, based on this letter?

Notice the voice change in v.6 from third person (he) to the first person (we). The voice shifted back in chapter 16 when Paul left Philippi. Now in 20:6, when Paul passed through Philippi on his way back to Troas, it shifts back to "we." From that evidence it is safe to say that Paul left Luke in Phillipi, probably to work with Lydia in the church that met in her house. Now Luke will be Paul's traveling companion until the end of the story.

Look at the list of Paul's traveling companions and plot on a map where they were from. What geographical regions does this group represent?

Why did Paul talk all night?

Why did the young man fall asleep?

What miracle happened that night?

A Final Sweep of the Aegean

Here are some observations from today's reading:

1. **Another divine detour.** The first detour we saw was when Paul was kept by the Holy Spirit from entering Asia. That was God directly saying, "No!" In today's reading we see that Paul was not allowed to sail directly to Jerusalem from Corinth because of a plot that the Jews had against his life. (Notice that the shield of protection in Corinth was now removed). Instead of sailing south, he headed north and retraced his steps through Macedonia. If we were Paul, once again, we would have probably asked, "Why, Lord? Why can't I go directly to Jerusalem and do the thing that you want me to do?" We can't know the definitive answer to that question in this circumstance, but we can make some observations. Had Paul not retraced his steps, he may not have reconnected with Luke in Philippi. Had Luke not rejoined Paul and traveled to Jerusalem he may have not have written the Gospel of Luke and the book of Acts. Had Paul not retraced his steps he may have never had the tearful farewell on the beach with the Ephesian leaders that we will read about tomorrow. The church is a richer place because of this divine detour. It is important for us to understand that everything – whether instigated by God directly or a plot of the enemy – can be used as an opportunity to bring about good for the Kingdom of God.

2. **The Gentile troops.** It is no accident that Luke highlighted the origin of each of Paul's traveling party. He did this to further demonstrate one of Paul's major themes; the unity of the body. Jerusalem was the mother church. It was the church where it all started. It was the church that came to the edge of denying the Gentiles equal fellowship with Jewish believers. Now the Jerusalem church was in trouble. It could have been tempting for the Gentile churches to think, "Serves them right. Let them suffer a little and see what it feels like," and further widen the ethnic division in the global body of Christ. Instead, Paul takes an aggressive stance and draws together a band of disciples, each representing the various regions

Acts: The Church is Born

Session 9: Finishing in Greece

in which he has planted churches, and takes them to Jerusalem. Through this act of humility, service, and even risk of personal harm, Paul was demonstrating to the church in Jerusalem, and to the church today, that unity in the body is of the highest importance for the health of the Kingdom of God.

Just for Kids

Today is another map day.

As you read the section show with arrows the path that Paul and his buddies took on the trip.

As you read the list of Paul's traveling companions, mark on your map where each of them are from. How does their hometown match up with the journeys that Paul has taken so far?

Acts: The Church is Born

Session 9: Finishing in Greece

Lesson 5

Acts 20:13-38

Why did Paul want to sail past Asia? What memories and connections did he have there?

How does Paul describe his experience in Asia? (vv. 18-21)

What was his message there?

In v. 22, the phrase translated "compelled by the Spirit" is the Greek phrase "dedemenos to pneumati" which literally means "having been bound or tied up in, or by, the Spirit". Read the following translations of this verse:

> And now, behold, I am going to Jerusalem, constrained by the Spirit, not knowing what will happen to me there, (English Standard Version)

> And now, behold, I go bound in the spirit unto Jerusalem, not knowing the things that shall befall me there (King James Version)

> "And now, behold, bound in spirit, I am on my way to Jerusalem, not knowing what will happen to me there (New American Standard Bible)

> "And now, compelled by the Spirit, I am going to Jerusalem, not knowing what will happen to me there. (New International Version)

> And now, as a captive to the Spirit, I am on my way to Jerusalem, not knowing what will happen to me there, (New Revised Standard Version)

In light of this phrase, how would you describe Paul's relationship with the Spirit? Is this the Holy Spirit, or his own spirit?

How does Paul view his immediate future? (vv. 22-24)

Paraphrase Paul's instructions to the elders in your own words. What were they supposed to do? How were they supposed to be? (vv. 28-35)

Based upon this story, how would you describe the relationship Paul had with the elders of Ephesus? (especially vv. 36-38)

Acts: The Church is Born

Session 9: Finishing in Greece

Leaders Learning Lessons

Today let's focus on leadership in the church. Whether you are an elder in the church and responsible for the flock within your local congregation, or you are a parent and responsible for the flock within your household, or a leader in your place of work, Paul's instructions are excellent guidelines for leadership.

1. **Keep Watch.** The Greek word being translated here is "prosecho" which means: to turn one's mind to, pay attention to, give heed to. It's not the sense of "Watch out! Because someone is coming after you." It's the sense of "be careful to pay close attention to." Notice the order of importance for being watchful. First keep watch of yourself, and then keep watch of others. The first rule of being a spiritual shepherd is to make sure that you are healthy. Make sure that you are daily being filled with God's Word and cleansed by God's Spirit. Make sure that your time and physical resources are managed well so that you do not fall into a trap of distraction or disease. Remember, if you are not healthy, you will not be able to shepherd others. Then, in the same way that you have watched over the daily disciplines of Bible study, prayer, worship, service, fellowship, and evangelism (Mind, Spirit, Body, Church, World) in your own life, be sure to instruct, equip, and encourage those in your flock to do the same. In v. 28, the NIV starts a new sentence with the imperative "Be shepherds" as if it were a new thought. The NASB translates it more closely to the Greek when it says,

   > "Be on guard for yourselves and for all the flock, among which the Holy Spirit has made you overseers, to shepherd the church of God which He purchased with His own blood."

   In other words, the leaders should take care of themselves and the flock, because that is what shepherding really is in the first place; it's watching out for the wellbeing of the sheep. Feed them, water them, and guide them.

2. **Stay Awake!** The word translated "be on your guard" is the Greek word "greigoreo" which means "keep awake, watch out". Paul reminds the elders that there are many wolves that surround the flock (some are even within the flock in sheep's clothing) that are just waiting for the moment when they can pounce on the weak and tear them to shreds. Here's one thing to keep in mind about the enemy. The enemy is very patient. Just like a crouching lion, the enemy of the church will wait…and wait…and even play soft lullabies…and wait…until the shepherd has become complacent and has nodded off to sleep. Then, WHAM! He pounces on the weak and unaware and drags them off. All because the shepherd fell asleep on his watch. Jesus warned the disciples many times to stay awake and keep watch. Now Paul repeats the command. As leaders of God's flock it is the elders' responsibility to always be aware of the threat of the enemy. We must pray diligently and not get lulled into complacency and apathy. We must never allow the sheep to stray or play near the edge of the woods. Stay awake!

You could summarize Paul's instructions to the elders like this, "Keep Watch and Watch Out." Or, "Take Care and Beware," or "Feed and Heed." Pick whichever catchy phrase you want. The point is that there is a great responsibility placed upon leadership in the church. If you are a leader, then take heed. If you are a sheep, pray for your shepherd and trust in the one Good Shepherd, Jesus.

Acts: The Church is Born

Session 9: Finishing in Greece

Just for Kids

Let's draw a picture today. Paul told the elders of Ephesus that they were shepherds. He told them to do two things as shepherds of God's Flock

1. **Take care of the sheep and watch over them.** What kind of things does the shepherd do to care for sheep? How can an elder of the church do these things for the church?

2. **Guard the flock.** There are lots of wolves that would love to steal and eat the little sheep in the flock. The shepherd has to make sure he always pays attention to keep the wolves out. What kind of wolves threaten the church? How can an elder protect against them?

Draw a picture of a shepherd taking care of and guarding the flock.

Maybe you could give the drawing to an elder as an encouragement to them.

Footnotes

[1] Carson, D. A. (1994). *New Bible commentary : 21st century edition.* Rev. ed. of: The new Bible commentary. 3rd ed. / edited by D. Guthrie, J.A. Motyer. 1970. (4th ed.) (Ac 19:23). Leicester, England; Downers Grove, Ill., USA: Inter-Varsity Press.

[2] Wood, D. R. W. (1996). *New Bible dictionary* (3rd ed. /) (Pages 86-87). Leicester, England; Downers Grove, Ill.: InterVarsity Press.

[3] Keener, C. S. (1993). *The IVP Bible background commentary : New Testament* (Ac 19:23). Downers Grove, Ill.: InterVarsity Press.

[4] Wood, D. R. W. (1996). *New Bible dictionary* (3rd ed. /) (Pages 86-87). Leicester, England; Downers Grove, Ill.: InterVarsity Press.

Acts: The Church is Born

Acts: The Church is Born

Session 10: A Mob in Jerusalem

Introduction

This week marks a stark change in the flow of Acts. Paul is done being a traveling missionary. The tree has spread its branches across the world and established new, Gentile root centers in Corinth and Ephesus. Now it is time for the circle to be completed as Paul returns to Jerusalem.

This week we turn to a new chapter in the story as we focus on Paul as a prisoner. After leaving the Aegean Sea, Paul, under the compulsion of the Holy Spirit, sailed to Syria, and then moved on to Jerusalem. Despite the passionate pleas of his friends, Paul was determined to face whatever harm may come to him in Jerusalem.

Agabus the prophet, through a prophetic pantomime, warned Paul that he would be bound in Jerusalem. James, the leader of the church in Jerusalem, warned Paul that the Jewish Christians were hostile toward him, and encouraged him to cleanse himself in a temple ritual. Despite his attempts to reenter the Jerusalem culture, Paul was misunderstood, and, like Jesus so many years before, was falsely accused and wrongfully arrested. It was only by the "grace" and protection of Rome that Paul was quite literally snatched from the hands of an angry and murderous mob. The fact that Paul was a citizen of Rome saved his life and set him up for the next journey in his life.

Acts: The Church is Born

Session 10: A Mob in Jerusalem

Lesson 1

Acts 21:1-16

Use your map and plot Paul's course as it is laid out in this passage.

Compare v. 4 with Acts 20:22-23. Do you see a difficulty? If so, how would you reconcile these two passages?

What do we know about Philip from the earlier part of Acts? How long has it been since those events?

Paraphrase the discussion between Paul and the rest of the group found in vv. 10-14. How would you describe the emotions in this scene? Why?

A Family in Every Port

One observation that we can make from this passage is that, once Paul landed in Syria, he found Christian fellowship in every city. Think about that for a minute. That's a miracle in itself. That is the kind of connectedness that most people deeply crave in their life. Wouldn't you like to be able to walk into any city and find friendly faces that would welcome you in, feed you, and treat you like family? In our sin-sick world, most people feel the isolating effects of the separation from God and others that the fall brought on humanity. The majority of people in the world feel lonely and isolated in the world and when they think about the entire globe they feel small and insignificant; alone in a vast cosmos. But not the child of God. As a follower of Jesus, we have been adopted into his great family and we have brothers and sisters all over the planet. The truth is that you can walk into most cities and find a group of Jesus followers and, simply through the name of Jesus, find an instant connection. You may have a different language, different social customs, and different theological nuances, but the bottom line is that you share the headship of Jesus and the Fatherhood of God. Through the bond of the Holy Spirit you can have true fellowship. That is a miracle. Let's never forget the global connection that we are privileged to share with people all over the world.

Conflicting messages?

Today we run into an apparent contradiction within the leadership of the Holy Spirit. In 20:22-23, Paul said that the Holy Spirit told him to go to Jerusalem and warned him that it would be difficult for him there. Now, in both Tyre and in Caesarea we find prophets who are "in the Spirit" that are urging Paul not to go to Jerusalem. So which is it? Is the Spirit telling Paul to go to Jerusalem, or is he telling him not to go? Is Paul a brave man who sticks to his guns regardless of what people say, or is he a stubborn mule who won't listen to the Holy Spirit and the advice of his friends?

The following commentaries deal with this well:

> I think we should begin by affirming that Luke believed Paul to be right in going to Jerusalem. Probably he attributes to the Holy Spirit both the decision of 19:21 and the compulsion of 20:22, since both of them were (enoto pneumati, "in

Acts: The Church is Born

Session 10: A Mob in Jerusalem

the Spirit'. In addition, we have already suggested that Luke sees Paul's journey to Jerusalem as the disciple following in his Master's footsteps. What then are we to make of 21:4 and 11? Some have argued that the references to the Spirit here simply mean that the speakers were claiming inspiration, without necessarily being inspired. But then we would have to interpret other references to the Spirit in the same ambiguous way. The better solution is to draw a distinction between a prediction and a prohibition. Certainly Agabus only predicted that Paul would be bound and handed over to the Gentiles (21:11); the pleadings with Paul which followed are not attributed to the Spirit and may have been the fallible (indeed mistaken) human deduction from the Spirit's prophecy. For if Paul had heeded his friends' pleas, then Agabus' prophecy would not have been fulfilled! It is more difficult to understand 21:4 in this way, since the 'urging' itself is said to be 'through the Spirit'. But perhaps Luke's' statement is a condensed way of saying that the warning was divine while the urging was human. After all, the Spirit's word to Paul combined the compulsion to go with a warning of the consequences. (20:22-23).[1]

The prophecy triggers an interaction between Paul and his fellow believers, including members of his traveling band. With tender affection the believers *pleaded* (better, "were pleading," imperfect) *with Paul not to go up* (better as a present prohibition, "cease going up"; Bruce 1990:442) *to Jerusalem* (compare 20:37–38; 21:4). They want to preserve the beloved apostle from physical harm, possibly death, and so keep him for themselves and the church's mission.

Paul responds with unwavering determination as he seeks to help them sort out the will of God in this matter. In such a process he recognizes the effects of their emotions on him. They are *weeping* for him as the women did for Jesus on the way to the cross (Lk 23:28). They are *breaking [his] heart,* his resolve, as stone is pulverized. He reaches back for the rationale that guides his whole life: *for the name of the Lord Jesus.* The One under whom he serves (Acts 20:19, 24) and in whose name he preaches, heals and baptizes (9:27–28; 16:18; 18:15; 19:5) is the One for whose name he is willing to suffer, even die (9:16; compare Lk 21:12; Acts 5:41). He reaffirms his resolve: he is *ready ... to be bound* (21:33) and, like the prophets and Jesus before him, *to die in Jerusalem* (Lk 13:33–34).

In devout resignation, unable to persuade him otherwise, they *gave up* (literally, "became quiet"; Lk 14:4; Acts 11:18), saying the only thing a Christian can say in such perplexing circumstances: *The Lord's will be done* (Lk 22:42).

We learn from Paul that suffering for the right reason, for the Lord's sake, is the key to a determination that correctly sorts out God's will. From the Christians we are instructed positively and negatively. Negatively, we must ask ourselves, "Has our own fear of radical obedience ever prompted us to crush someone else's determination to do the Lord's will? Has tender affection ever been substituted for courageous love in wanting God's best for someone else?" (Ogilvie 1983:298). Positively, do we know when to cease striving with one another and in humility, recognizing our lack of definitive knowledge of God's plan for the other, start asking God to carry out his desire for their lives?[2]

Acts: The Church is Born

Session 10: A Mob in Jerusalem

Just for Kids

First, let's get out our maps again. Draw arrows that show Paul's movements in this passage. Label the places mentioned in the text on your map.

Let's act out the scene.

Find a rope or a belt from a bathrobe. Have one person pretend to be Agabus. Another person needs to tie Agabus' hands together at the wrists.

Agabus says,

> "In this way the Jews of Jerusalem will bind the owner of this belt and will hand him over to the Gentiles."

In the Old Testament, prophets often acted out their message in this way to get the point across.

- Ahijah tore Jeroboam's cloak into 12 pieces (1 Kings 11:29ff)
- Isaiah went stripped and barefoot for three years (Isaiah 20:3ff)
- Ezekiel laid siege to a drawing of Jerusalem (Ezekiel 4:1ff)

Why do you think prophets taught like this?

What helps you to best remember a lesson that your teacher is trying to tell you? In other words, what is your learning style?

God uses all kinds of methods to get us to learn the things that are very important for us to remember. That's because God loves us so much and doesn't want us to miss out on anything.

Acts: The Church is Born

Session 10: A Mob in Jerusalem

Lesson 2

Acts 21:17-25

In light of the intense discussion from yesterday's reading, what kind of reception do you think Paul and his companions were expecting when they arrived in Jerusalem? What did they receive? (v. 17)

Read Acts 12:17 and 15:13. From these verses, what do we know about James? What was his role in the church in Jerusalem?

How did James respond to the news concerning the number of Gentiles that had come to follow Jesus?

How did James describe the Christian Jews?

What problem did the Christian Jews have with Paul?

What did James propose would be a good method to dissuade the Christian Jews from their ill feelings toward Paul? Why?

In v. 24-25 how does James describe the people's expectations for Paul? How does he describe their expectations for the Gentile believers?

Review Acts 15:19-29 to gain a better understanding for v. 25. What was the nature of the relationship between Jewish believers in Jerusalem and the Gentile believers in the rest of the world? In what ways can you see this type of relationship at play within the church in our own time, if any?

Acts: The Church is Born

Session 10: A Mob in Jerusalem

Coming Home

There is an old expression that states, "You can never go home." Here's a typical scenario of why that is true. A high school graduate has lived in a small town his whole life. He's gone to school and to church with the same group of people. It was a good life and his church and friends were good people. Then one day he goes off to college in the big city. His experiences there rock his world. He is exposed to new cultures and new ideas. His faith is challenged at the genetic level and God opens his eyes up to whole new vistas of opportunity for what it means to be a global Christian. He is filled with exuberance and has a perspective for ministry that is beyond what he thought it could ever be.

And then he returns home. As he drives into the city limits he feels like he has entered a time warp. There's the old drug store with the same man sitting in the same rocking chair. There's the church with the same cars parked in the same spots. As he enters church on Sunday morning it seems that everyone is moving in slow motion and the air is filled with a dusty staleness. The people look at his wild hair style and his clothes and begin to murmur to each other. Old friends reach out a hand to shake his, and behind their pasted smile, their eyes say, "Wow, you have gone off the deep end, haven't you?"

There is an awkwardness that gives him pause to question what has happened. This is my home, but why do I feel like I don't belong?

At that point the young man has a choice to make. Does he exercise the new found freedoms that he has discovered in his travels, or does he conform to the patterns of his home in order to keep the peace? If he conforms, will he be betraying himself and become hypocritical by caving into the pressure of these backward religious systems. Or, will he be demonstrating love for his hometown people by not needlessly ruffling their feathers and causing a ruckus, thus distracting them from the worship that they came to give God.

This may have been some of the feelings that Paul experienced as he came back into Jerusalem. He was warmly greeted by James, which was a nice surprise, given the harsh warnings he had been hearing leading up to this arrival. Yet, quickly James warned him that the people of Jerusalem, the believers even, were uneasy about some of Paul's teachings. They were confused about his interaction with Gentiles. It was so far outside their paradigm that they did not know how to deal with it, or him. The believers knew about the decision of the Jerusalem council regarding the fact that Gentiles need not be circumcised to be saved, but they still didn't know how to handle it.

James encouraged Paul to enter into a Jewish rite of cleansing in order to demonstrate to the Jews that he was not a lawbreaker and was in line with the teachings of Moses. What!?! How could James ask such a thing? Wouldn't that be hypocritical of Paul to do such a thing? After all, Paul does not believe that the Law does us any good other than to expose our sin and need for grace, right?

Notice what Paul does. He doesn't even bat an eye at James' request. He very willingly enters into the purification rite. Why does he do this? Paul does it for one reason...unity. That is the main theme in this whole story. Paul's mission was to bridge the prejudicial gap that stood between the Jews and the Gentiles. Paul wasn't out to stand up for Paul. He wasn't about saving his own dignity or being "right." Paul was demonstrating true love; God's absolute love for God's people. God's love transcends denominational and doctrinal differences and unifies the body of Christ under the Father, in the name of Jesus, through the bond of the Spirit. For Paul it always came down to one thing; the name of Jesus. Nothing more. If he was in Ephesus he could base his operation out of a Greek lecture hall. If he was in Jerusalem he could shave his head in the purification rite of the Nazirites and pay for four others to do the same. As long as he could preach Jesus, he was good with whatever culture he was in.

We can never go home. That is true. Yet, we must also remember that the only home we have is the Kingdom of God. The great thing about the Kingdom is that you can be there wherever you are. So, we can never go home, because we are always there.

Acts: The Church is Born

Session 10: A Mob in Jerusalem

Just for Kids

Does your family have certain rules about how to behave in your house? For example: do you have to take off your shoes before you walk on the carpet? Do you have to all sit together at the dinner table and no one can leave until they ask to be excused? Do you have a specific bedtime? Do you have special family nights and traditions that are really important to your family?

Would you expect every family to share your exact rules? Why or why not?

Let's pretend that your family was going to a different country and you were going to have dinner in the home of a village chief. When you were there, would expect the chief to follow your house rules or would you be expected to follow his house rules? Why?

What do you think would happen if the village chief expected you to take off your shoes, bow in honor to him, and eat the hors d'ouvers, but, instead, you tromped across his floor with dirty shoes, slapped him on the back, and exclaimed, "I wouldn't touch that slop with a ten foot pole!"? Would the rest of your evening go well? Why?

In the story today, Paul came back to Jerusalem, where everyone followed a lot of specific rules. While Paul was in Asia and Greece, witnessing about Jesus to the Greeks, these rules didn't seem that important. Paul knew the rules weren't necessary in order to know Jesus and be a part of the Kingdom of God. Yet, Paul also knew that it was proper to respect the "house rules" of Jerusalem and make sure that he didn't offend anybody. That's because the most important thing in the body of Christ is that we live in peace and unity with each other, under the leadership of Jesus.

The lesson for us is to make sure that we don't offend someone for no good reason, especially if it would give Jesus a bad name in that house.

Acts: The Church is Born

Session 10: A Mob in Jerusalem

Lesson 3

Acts 21:26-39

Read the following commentary to gain context for this scene:

> The church leaders counsel Paul to combat words with action. Four pious but indigent men in the congregation have taken on themselves a Nazirite vow of limited duration (Num 6). By abstaining from products of the vine, not cutting their hair and avoiding ritual impurity, they have been showing thankfulness for past blessings, earnestness in petition or strong devotion to God. The multianimal sacrifice and cleansing ceremony at the end of the vow period, when the hair is cut and offered to God, is financially prohibitive (6:13–20). Paul is asked to bear the expenses of the four. This was a commonly recognized act of piety (Josephus Jewish Antiquities 19.294). To do so he must go through a seven-day ritual cleansing himself, because he has recently returned from Gentile lands (m. Oholot 2:3; 17:5; 18:6; Num 19:12). The intended result is that the rumors about Paul will be shown to be baseless and he will be seen living in obedience to the law. Lest Paul's action be misunderstood in another direction, as making Jewish custom normative for Gentile Christians, the elders hasten to add that the Jerusalem Council decree is still in place (see discussion above at Acts 15:20, 29). It is repeated here in essential detail.³

What two accusations were brought against Paul? One was regarding his teaching; the other was regarding his current action.

Read the following commentary to gain context on the second accusation:

> Though Gentiles were welcome to worship in the outermost court, they were forbidden on penalty of death to enter beyond the balustrade into the two inner courts (m. Kelim 1:8). Josephus informs us, and archaeological evidence confirms, that at intervals there were signs posted in Greek and Latin saying "No foreigner is to enter within the forecourt and the balustrade around the Sanctuary. Whoever is caught will have himself to blame for his subsequent death" (Segal 1989:79; Polhill [1992:452] has information on the present location of such an inscription; Josephus Jewish Wars 5.193). This prohibition enforced Numbers 3:38.⁴

Why did the mob attack and beat Paul?

What stopped the mob? Why?

What preconception did the commander have regarding Paul? How might this have affected his treatment of Paul?

Read Luke 23:13-25. Do you see any parallels to this story?

Acts: The Church is Born

Session 10: A Mob in Jerusalem

The Power of Prejudice

There is great irony in this passage. Yesterday we discussed how Paul had transcended the Jewish religious system as he was called to the Gentiles. Yet, truly, Paul had never left his Jewish roots. He was a Pharisee at the core. That was his natural love language for God. He probably cherished that day when he was able to reenter the Temple to be cleansed before God. This was good and natural for him. As he went through these rituals he was not only truly connecting to his roots, he was also authentically demonstrating his humility and his love for the Jewish people.

That is where the irony comes into play. The Jewish people were not seeking the truth. They had a preconceived idea about what they assumed Paul was all about. Let's look at it through their eyes for a minute. Here is a man that was once one of them. Then, one day, he just ups and leaves and starts hanging out with Gentiles. There is no way that a man that was once a staunch Pharisee could possibly still love the ways of the Temple and the Law after having spent so much time with Gentiles. For them it was a black and white issue. It was either/or. You were either a Pharisee and hated all Gentiles, or you were a total apostate and deserved to be thrown out to the dogs.

That's what happens when we carry around our own perspective as if it were the infallible source of all truth. Prejudice has blinded the eyes of many well meaning people. Of course, in our own country, we have seen the devastating effects of racial prejudice on the lives of people in the 20th century. It was no different in Jerusalem. The Jews saw Paul the way they wanted to see him and were not willing to take the time to find out the truth about his position.

James, no doubt, stood in the streets that day and watched as the crowd nearly killed Paul. Perhaps that is why he wrote the words,

> "My dear brothers, take note of this: Everyone should be quick to listen, slow to speak and slow to become angry, for man's anger does not bring about the righteous life that God desires." (James 1:19-20)

We can learn from this story. Too many times we tend to jump to conclusions about a person's behavior and assume the worst. If we have built up a negative belief about someone, then we will have a very difficult time seeing the truth in that person's life. If you believe someone doesn't like you, then you will interpret every word they say to you as some sort of attack. Even if it is an honest compliment. If you believe someone is a liar, then you will hear everything they say as a lie. If you believe someone is lazy, then you will interpret even their best efforts as a slack-off.

The path of growth for us in this is to 1) admit that we have built a prejudice against someone. 2) Acknowledge the fact that a prejudice, or negative belief, is a form of judging that person, and that judging a person is to presume the place of God in their life. That is idolatry because you have placed yourself on God's throne because only God has the right to judge. 3) Confess that sin to God, turn away from it, and receive God's forgiveness that is readily given to the repentant heart. 4) Ask God to give you the wisdom, patience, and discernment to truly seek first to understand that person for who they really are and discover what the truth is in every situation. 5) Be willing to be wrong in your own perspective and teachable if that person has something to offer.

Don't let the pride of being right or the fear of being wrong stand in your way of growing closer to God and to each other. If we, in the church, could learn to do that, then we would have much less strife in our lives and the Kingdom of God would be given freedom to flourish more readily in our hearts and the world.

Acts: The Church is Born

Session 10: A Mob in Jerusalem

Just for Kids

What does the word prejudice mean? If you're not sure, look it up in the dictionary.

Let's do a little experiment. Have one person leave the room so that they don't hear these instructions. If they hear them, then it won't be any fun for anybody.

Instructions

We are going to trick the person who has left the room and make them think that we are doing a taste test to see which is a better drink between two products. You can do this one of two ways. You can either do it with soda or with juices.

Soda method.

> Put a soda in one cup and lemon juice in the other cup.
>> Blindfold the person who left the room and set them down in front of the two cups. Tell them,
>>> "Today we are going to do a test to see which is sweeter, Soda A or Soda B."
>>
>> Hand them "Soda A" (which is the actual soda) and have them drink it. They should enjoy it.
>>
>> Then hand them "Soda B" (which is actually the lemon juice) and say, "Now tell us if soda B is as sweet as or sweeter than soda A" Have them drink the lemon juice and see what happens.

Juice method.

> Do exactly the same as in the soda method, except have it be a comparison between sweet fruit juices, like apple vs. grape.

Obviously the person will react strongly to the lemon juice.

Follow up questions:

Why did (s)he react so strongly to the lemon juice? What was (s)he expecting?

You see, (s)he had a prejudice about the experiment. He thought that the drink was going to be sweet, but it wasn't. Had he been expecting lemon juice (s)he may have reacted differently.

In our story today, the Jews and the Roman commander had a prejudice against Paul. The Jews thought that he was rebelling against Moses and teaching Jews to stop being Jewish. The Roman commander thought Paul was an Egyptian rebel. In both cases these incorrect assumptions about Paul led the people to treat Paul cruelly, almost to the point of killing him.

In what ways does prejudice impact our society? How can we work against the negative impact of prejudice?

Acts: The Church is Born

Session 10: A Mob in Jerusalem

Lesson 4

Acts 21:40-22:21

Why do you suppose Paul's Aramaic brought silence to the crowd? (note that the native tongue of Jerusalem was Aramaic)

How does Paul describe himself before his encounter with Jesus?

Paraphrase Paul's encounter with Jesus in your own words.

How is Ananias described?

In v. 14, how is God described?

In vv. 14-16, what is Paul commissioned to do?

Where was Paul when he received his vision that is described in vv. 17-21?

Why did Paul have to leave Jerusalem?

Where was Paul sent?

Paul's Testimony

Here are some observations concerning Paul's testimony.

He spoke Aramaic. As always, he was culturally relevant. When Paul was in Greece, he spoke Greek and quoted Greek poetry. When he was in Jerusalem he spoke Aramaic, which was the language of his people. Paul's ultimate goal was to communicate the truth of Jesus in the most effective way, that followed the path of least resistance, while maintaining the purity of the message; the risen Jesus.

No one could question his zeal. Paul makes it a point to highlight the fact that, in this very city, he was even more zealous for the Law than this mob was being in that moment. Paul was so zealous that he even hunted down followers of the Way in other cities in order to bring them to justice and eradicate this plague. Paul highlighted this for two reasons. First, he wanted to remind the mob that, deep down, he was actually one of them; he was not a foreigner. Secondly, he wanted to point out that if anybody was the least likely candidate to be turned to the Way it would be him. In other words, if Paul followed Jesus, then his experience must have been authentic.

It was a person, not a persuasion. This is a very important point in the study and ministry of Paul. Saul of Tarsus did not fall under the spell of a great teacher, like Peter, and become intellectually persuaded that Jesus from Nazareth was the Messiah. Had that been the case then the power of his message, and more importantly, his resolve to press on in the midst of terrible circumstances would have been easily abated. It is the fact that Saul of Tarsus encountered the risen Jesus, in all his glory, power, and authority, that stands as the center piece of Paul's message. This personal encounter transformed Saul in that moment. It changed him from an Old Testament Pharisee, seeking to liberate Israel through the observance of the Law, to a fulfilled child of Abraham, liberated by the victorious King of the Jews. The Kingdom of God that Saul had so desperately longed for, and the end of the world that he believed would bring justice on the world, had become fully realized in the person of the risen Jesus. That is a fact that Paul presented to the mob and could never, ever deny.

Acts: The Church is Born

Session 10: A Mob in Jerusalem

The first disciples of Jesus deeply loved the Law. Paul specifically highlights the fact that Ananias, his first contact with the brotherhood of the church, was deeply devoted to the Law. This flew in the face of the prejudices that Saul was carrying with him on his crusade to Damascus. In Saul's case, he had misunderstood the followers of the Way. So, too, in the case of the mob, was Paul misunderstood.

His mission began in the Temple. It was no accident that Paul highlighted the fact that his marching orders to take the Good News of Jesus to the Gentiles came to him while he was in trance while praying in the Temple. Even after his conversion to Jesus, Paul did not turn away from the Temple. He was simply commanded to go to the ends of the earth by the risen Jesus that had changed his life and taken authority.

He was the bridge. The thing that the Jews hated most about Paul was that his message taught that, in God's eyes, all people are equal, regardless of their race or gender. This flew in the face of all of their theology. They were an exclusive club of "the circumcision" and God loved them and no one else. Paul's talk of non-circumcised citizens of God's Kingdom could not fit into their paradigm. And yet, that is exactly what Paul was sent to proclaim and demonstrate. God had torn down the dividing wall and Paul was the human conduit that stood in the gap. Paul was not hated and threatened for the name of Jesus, he was hated because he taught that Gentiles were welcomed by God.

Just for Kids

Let's draw a picture today. Take a piece of paper and divide it into three columns. At the top of the left column, write the words "Paul before Jesus". At the top of the middle column write the words, "Paul meets Jesus." At the top of the third column, write the words, "Paul after Jesus."

Based on Paul's testimony in today's reading, draw a picture that describes him in each of these three places in his life.

Acts: The Church is Born

Session 10: A Mob in Jerusalem

Lesson 5

Acts 22:22-29

How did the crowd respond to Paul's testimony?

What set them off? (v. 21)

What saved Paul from being flogged by the Romans?

Read the following passages and make observations regarding the relationship between Paul and the Roman Government.

Acts 13:4-12

Acts 16:35-40

Acts 18:12-17

Acts 19:28-41

In each of these encounters, compare and contrast the Jewish leader's relationship with Paul with that of the Roman officials.

A Life-Saving ID

In today's reading Paul pulled his ultimate trump card. He was a Roman citizen. Because of that fact, he could not be abused by the Roman soldiers without a trial. It was his citizenship in Rome that actually saved his life.

At this point let us step back from the story itself and look at the book of Acts as the document that came from Luke's hand. Every biblical author wrote their work with an agenda. Luke is no exception. Luke wrote the Gospel of Luke and the Acts of the Apostles with some very specific theological, political, and sociological agendas in mind. The most obvious of these agendas, of course, was to demonstrate the historical reliability of the life of Jesus and to present Jesus of Nazareth as the legitimate Christ, on the throne of God's Kingdom, and victor over sin and death.

While the supremacy of Jesus is the most important theme, there are two other themes that should be highlighted at this point. First, Luke was setting out to launch a counter-attack against the opponents of Paul that accused him of being an illegitimate apostle. The circumcision group that followed Paul into nearly every town in which he planted churches claimed that only the Hebraic Jewish apostles that were part of the original twelve were legitimate apostles and that Paul's message of Gentile equality and liberty was apostate. Luke, a dear friend and disciple of Paul, spent a great deal of energy in Acts carefully dismantling this accusation through the life and circumstances of Paul. That is why Paul is the dominant character of Acts.

The second theme has to do with the relationship between Rome and the church. In the 60s there was growing unrest between the Roman Empire and the Jewish nation. Eventually, in A.D. 70 Rome would come down on Israel and brutally crush Jerusalem and level the Temple, never to be restored. It was during the decade or so leading up to that event that Luke wrote Luke/Acts. Early in its history, the followers of the Way were considered to be simply another sect of Judaism by the Roman government. In its inception this was a very positive thing for the early church since it kept them off the radar of the Empire and under the protection that the Jews experienced at that time. As things grew worse for the Jews it was important that the church separate itself from

Acts: The Church is Born

Session 10: A Mob in Jerusalem

them in the eyes of Rome. If the Romans were going to persecute Christians for the name of Jesus, that was fine, but they should not be persecuted in the name of the Jewish religious system. Therefore, as you saw in the study questions, Luke took special effort to highlight the fact that Rome had always looked favorably, or at worst neutrally, upon the followers of Jesus. Now, in today's reading, once again, we see that it was actually Rome that saved Paul's life. His subsequent imprisonment in Caesarea and house arrest in Rome was, while inconvenient, not a brutal torture chamber or dungeon experience. It actually was a safety nest that kept him physically safe from a murderous mob.

As we come to the end of this week, it could be easy to say, "So what? We've learned some neat factoids about Paul and Acts, but what does it have to do with my life today?" Good question. Here's the take home for the week. When we analyze Paul's life it becomes obvious that Paul was not concerned about human political systems or socio-economic status. Paul didn't care if he was in Greece or in Jerusalem. He didn't care if he was being lauded as a hero or hunted as a criminal. None of that made any difference to him. The only thing that mattered to him was that the name of Jesus, that risen Lord who he met on the road, was being proclaimed to the world and that all people were given opportunity to enter into the Kingdom of God. It is all about Jesus, the risen King, and nothing else. The same should be true about our lives and ministry. As soon as we take our eyes off of Jesus and start worrying about political parties and agendas, or theological distinctives, or the "in" group, it is at that point that we open the back door of the Kingdom and allow the enemy to enter in and start setting up his strongholds of deception, destruction, and divisiveness in the church. Let's make sure we never forget that Jesus is the head of the church, we serve him, and he leads us all in the way that he desires us to be led.

Just for Kids

A big question that comes up for followers of Jesus has to do with how we should treat the government of our country. Since Jesus is our King and we live in the Kingdom of God, do we have to obey the laws of our country?

Read Romans 13:1-7 and 1 Peter 2:13-17 to see how both Paul and Peter answered this question.

Based on these passages, how should a follower of Jesus treat their country? When would be the only time it would be right to break the law of your country?

(Footnotes)

[1] Stott, John. The Message of Acts. The Bible Speaks Today Commentary. Intervarsity Press. 1990. (p. 333)

[2] Larkin, W. J., Briscoe, D. S., & Robinson, H. W. (1995). *Vol. 5: Acts*. The IVP New Testament commentary series (Ac 21:7). Downers, Ill., USA: InterVarsity Press.

[3] ibid (Ac 21:23).

[4] ibid (Ac 21:30).

Acts: The Church is Born

Session 11: Paul on Trial

Introduction

This week we see Paul, and the Gospel message itself, on trial. Many accusations had been brought against "the Way" in the few decades that it had been around. The Jews accused it of undermining Judaism and blaspheming against Moses, the Law, the Prophets, and, ultimately, against God. The Greek and Roman citizens had accused it of undermining the authority of Rome and Caesar. They said that the Christians were advocating political upheaval and revolt so that their Jesus could become the king.

As Luke penned these words he was presenting an apologetic – a defense – against these unfounded and dangerous accusations. As Paul stands before the Sanhedrin, we see that the Jews had no case against the Way and were so divided amongst themselves that they were no longer capable of leading God's people. As Paul stands before Felix and Festus, we see that the Christians were not only *not* against Rome, but that Rome, time and again, had actually come to Christian's aid and protection. Finally, as Paul stands before Agrippa, the Jewish king, we see that the person of Jesus, resurrected and victorious, is the actual King of the Jews and of the Kingdom that God had promised to Abraham.

Paul, the humbled and broken prisoner, was demonstrating that Jesus' Kingdom was not entangled in the affairs of this world but was calling all people, of every race and nation, to come into their eternal home.

Acts: The Church is Born

Session 11: Paul on Trial

Lesson 1

Acts 22:30-23:35

Why did the high priest have Paul struck?

How did Paul respond to this assault? Was this a proper response? Why or why not?

By quoting Exodus 22:28, what was Paul saying?

How did Paul identify himself in v. 6? In what tense was this spoken?

What caused the uproar in the assembly?

Compare this story with Acts 4:1-4ff. Who is the real antagonist in these stories? Why?

What promise did Jesus make to Paul? Why do you suppose Paul needed a special visitation from Jesus at this point?

What foiled the plot to ambush Paul?

Who is Paul's protector (on a human level) in this story?

Still a Pharisee

Three observations:

1. **Paul was still a Pharisee.** If you grew up in Sunday school, then the name "Pharisee" probably sends chills down your spine. The Pharisees are typically presented as the villainous foes of Jesus and the apostles. While it is true that, ultimately, they were opposed to the followers of the Way, it is important for us to see them in a truer light than this Sunday-schoolish caricature. If the Pharisees were evil, then how is it that Paul can identify himself, in the present tense, as a Pharisee? Either he was playing a manipulative trick to instigate a fight, or he was telling the truth. The former option is unlikely, so the latter must be true. Throughout this whole section we will see that Paul makes a strong case for the fact that he considered himself as much a Jew in the present circumstances as he ever was prior to his Jesus encounter. As we have discussed before, Paul did not leave his pharisaical belief system on the road to Damascus. Much to the contrary, his pharisaical beliefs were actually intensified when he met first-hand evidence of the core of his belief system: a resurrected Messiah. From that day forward, he was simply acting as a fulfilled Pharisee, living in the present reality of the eschatological (a fancy word for the end of time) Kingdom of God. While this may seem esoteric and not practical for today, there is something we can glean from it. To be a radical for Jesus does not mean to abandon tradition. It simply means to live in the fullness of tradition and use it for its intended purpose.

2. **Jerusalem was a dangerous place.** Luke is making a strong statement in these closing chapters of Acts. His statement was both political and theological. Theologically, he was reinforcing the idea that the "center of the universe" was shifting. For a millennium, the Jews had looked to Jerusalem as the geographical center of the universe and God's "Holy City." Now Luke was exposing that city for what it was; nothing more than a group of highly distracted leaders who had developed a very distorted lens that was obscuring their ability to see the truth of God's work. They were the keepers of God's vineyard that had forgotten about tending the vine and were now being replaced. No longer was Jerusalem the center, but the center is now the person of Jesus Christ. There is no geographical center. In fact, this is how it has always been. It was the human

Acts: The Church is Born

Session 11: Paul on Trial

distortion factor that centered on Jerusalem in the first place. Jesus, through his apostles, was simply restoring the Kingdom to what it was originally intended to be.

3. **Rome was Paul's protector.** Luke's political statement has to do with the apostle Paul's, specifically, and all Christians', generally, relationship with Rome. The book of Luke/Acts was, among other things, an apologetic to demonstrate that Christianity was not an enemy of the Empire, but was, quite the contrary, a movement that had always received sympathies from the Empire. This was true of Jesus and his relationship with Pilate, and it is true of the apostle Paul as well. Christians are not political revolutionaries. They are not of this world and they let the people of the world mess with the politics.

Just for Kids

Read the following verses.

Exodus 22:28

When someone speaks harshly to you, or falsely accuses you of something, what is your first reaction? What kind of things do you want to say back to them? Why?

In our story today we see that Paul lost his temper and spoke harshly to the high priest... That was wrong. Here are some lessons we can learn.

1. Even when someone is wrong, they still deserve to be treated with respect.
2. When you make a mistake – like losing your temper and speaking harshly – it is important to ask for forgiveness.

Acts: The Church is Born

Session 11: Paul on Trial

Lesson 2

Acts 24:1-27

Read the following dictionary article about Felix:

> he seems to have held the procuratorship of Judaea from c. ad 52. Unrest increased under his rule, for 'with savagery and lust he exercised the powers of a king with the disposition of a slave' (Tacitus,. Hist. 5. 9), and he was utterly merciless in crushing opposition. In c. ad 55 he put down the followers of a Messianic pretender of Egyptian origin, but the man himself escaped (Jos., BJ 2.261ff.). When the riot recorded in Acts 21:27ff. broke out the tribune Claudius Lysias initially mistook Paul for this *Egyptian (Acts 21:38).
>
> After his arrest Paul was conveyed to Caesarea, the Roman capital of Palestine, and was tried before Felix. Two well-attested characteristics of the governor stand out in the subsequent narrative: his disregard for justice and his avarice. He kept Paul in prison for 2 years, hoping he would be paid a fat bribe (Acts 24:26). Disappointed of this hope, he deferred judgment in a case where there was ample evidence of the prisoner's innocence (23:29), and upon his recall he left Paul in prison in order to please the Jews (24:27) or, according to the Western Text, to please his wife *Drusilla.
>
> He was recalled by Nero, probably in ad 59 (*Festus), and was saved from proceedings instigated by the Jews only through the influence of Pallas. Of Felix' later history nothing is known.[1]

In light of the above article, how would you describe Tertullus' opening statements to Felix?

What accusations were brought against Paul? Were any of them founded?

How does Paul describe himself in vv. 11-16?

What was Paul's purpose for coming to Jerusalem? What was his attitude toward Jerusalem and the Temple when he was there?

Read the following excerpt regarding Drusilla:

> Drusilla, the wife of Antonius Felix who was procurator of Judea (ca. a.d. 52-59) while Paul was imprisoned in Caesarea. A Jewess, she was the daughter of Herod Agrippa I and great-granddaughter of Herod the Great. Originally given in marriage to the Syrian Azizus of Emesa, she was apparently persuaded to leave him for Felix.[2]

What was the heart of Paul's message that was directed to Felix and Drusilla? How was it received?

Summarize Felix's dealings and attitudes toward Paul.

Acts: The Church is Born

Session 11: Paul on Trial

Caesarea: Before Felix

In Paul's defense statement to Felix, he highlights four things that have been true about his life. They have remained constant both before he met Jesus and after he met Jesus. Let's look at these four things, see how they should be true in our lives, and see how Jesus transformed and fulfilled them.

I worship God. In the Old Testament, the word for worship is interchangeable with "serve." Paul wasn't saying that he loved to have a hymn-sing all the time. He was saying that his primary focus was on God and bringing everything in his life into submission to his Lord. May that be true of our lives. May we be constant worshippers in everything that we do.

I believe everything that agrees with the Law and Prophets. Paul's understanding of God and the Kingdom was based upon the objective revelation of God through the scriptures. This is a very important component of a life devoted to God. Our understanding of God and our decisions are not based upon subjective ideas and/or notions. Rather, we are to be students of the Word of God so that we can know the very mind and heart of God and follow according to God's ways.

I have a hope in the resurrection. Hope is what inspires us and drives us to persevere through the most difficult of circumstances. Without hope we can become complacent and depressed even when things seem to be going well. It is the reality of the resurrection of the dead in the last day that gives our lives meaning. There is a finish line. There is a point and a purpose to everything. We are not just cosmic accidents that are drifting through a pointless mess of chaos, only to be snuffed out and forgotten in the end. We are eternal beings that look forward to the resurrection of both the righteous and the unrighteous, and an existence either in the presence of God or not.

I strive to keep my conscience clean. Given the hope that we have of the resurrection, suddenly there is now a reason for a system of morality. The Law stated that we are to love God and love our neighbors as ourselves. When we do this, then our consciences will be clean and we can stand before a Holy God, sanctified and presentable to God.

These things were true of Paul from the time he was a little child. It has always been God's plan for God's people. Then, one day, Paul, the Law-abiding, zealous-for-God Pharisee, met Jesus in his resurrected glory and everything changed. Suddenly each of these four points popped into a new level of clarity that plunged Paul into a deeper level of reality than he had ever known.

Now, through the Jesus lens...

He could worship God, not as a far-off creator, but as a loving heavenly Father. Now he knew the love of God through the person of Jesus and Paul's worship could be an authentic "attitude of gratitude" rather than merely a fearful and distant respect.

He could **understand the Old Testament** (the Law and the Prophets) as the pointer to the person of Jesus. He could see God's hand working through the history of Israel to prepare the way for the eternal Messiah. The scriptures jumped from black and white into living Technicolor!

His **hope in the resurrection** was no longer a desire for a far off reality. Now he had encountered the first-fruits of the resurrection and could actually live in the power of the resurrection that came through the indwelling Holy Spirit. His hope shifted from a future gaze to a present reality.

Now he actually had the power to **keep a clean conscience** before God. Before, he had to rely upon his own merit and his observance of the external ceremonial cleansing rituals to demonstrate his heart to God. No man can stay clean that way. But now, he has the great conscience cleaner, the Holy Spirit, living inside of him to sanctify him and purify him in ever increasing ways, to present him spotless before the Almighty God.

Just for Kids

In Paul's testimony to Governor Felix, he points out 4 things that are important for everyone to keep a part of their life. Take out a piece of paper, divide it into four sections and draw a picture of one in each section. They are:

Worship

Bible Study

Hope in Resurrection

Clear conscience.

Spend some time discussing what each of these four things means. How well does your life demonstrate these four areas?

Acts: The Church is Born

Session 11: Paul on Trial

Lesson 3

Acts 25:1-12

Read the following article describing Festus.

> FESTUS. Porcius Festus succeeded *Felix as procurator of Judaea. Nothing is known of his life before his appointment, and he died in office after about 2 years. In Josephus (Ant. 20.182ff. and BJ 2.271) he makes an agreeable contrast with his predecessor Felix and his successor Albinus. In Acts (24:27–26:32) he appears in a less favourable light. Though he tried Paul's case with commendable alacrity (25:6) and was convinced of his innocence (26:31), he was prepared to sacrifice Paul to do the Jews a pleasure (25:9). Hence the scandalous suggestion of retrial at Jerusalem. Paul was constrained to appeal to Caesar in the face of an arrangement which would have put him in the power of his enemies. Yet Festus was apparently baffled by Paul, and brought the case before Agrippa II and *Bernice. Paul's innocence emerges clearly in the sequel, but the appeal proceeds to Rome.
>
> Festus was later involved when the Jewish leaders brought to Nero a successful suit against Agrippa's violation of the privacy of the Temple area (Jos., Ant. 20.189ff.).
>
> The date of Festus' arrival in Judaea is a major crux of Pauline chronology. W. M. Ramsay in Pauline Studies, pp. 348ff., argued that Eusebius' evidence, when rightly understood, points to ad 59, and some support for this date is found in the sudden change of procuratorial coinage in that year, an event most plausibly attributed to the arrival of a new governor (see H. J. Cadbury, The Book of Acts in History, 1955, pp. 9f.).[3]

Why did the Jews want Paul to be transferred to Jerusalem?

Why did Paul appeal to Caesar? What was at stake?

Before Festus

Two observations today:

1. **Paul was willing to die, but not for the wrong reasons.** Festus, in an attempt to appease the Jews, asked Paul if he was willing to go to Jerusalem to stand trial. Paul wasn't an idiot. He knew that two years earlier 40 men had vowed not to eat or drink until they had killed Paul in an ambush (do you wonder if those guys starved to death...just asking!) Paul knew that the Jews had no case against him, other than the fact that they wanted him dead and out of the way. Acquiescing to Festus' proposal would be nothing short of suicide. If death was the only option then he was ready to face it, but there was another way. He had the Roman-citizen-get-out-of-the-gallows-free card to play. Since he was already in the Roman judicial system, and since he was a Roman citizen, he knew that if he appealed to Caesar, then Festus would be legally bound to send him to Rome and not to Jerusalem. Paul is saved and the Jews plot to kill him is foiled once again.

2. **Unexpected paths.** A running theme in Paul's life is that God has a tendency to mess with our plans. We saw it in his second journey. He was headed to Ephesus, but God sent him to Macedonia and on to Corinth. On his third journey he wanted to sail south to Syria from Corinth, but he was forced to head north to Philippi. We know that Paul had a strong desire to visit Rome and then to move further west into Spain. (Romans 15:24). It is safe to bet then, when he laid awake at night, envisioning his missionary trip to Rome, that he did not picture himself being chained between two Roman guards and stuck in the belly of a prison cell. Yet, when he appealed to Caesar, that is exactly what happened. Here's the take home for us. We saw it in his ministry in Ephesus, and we see it again here in his trip to Rome. God will work his plan in our lives, but very often it will look different than what we had planned. It is good to make plans, but we must always hold our plans with open hands and follow God in the way that he works out the details. In the end, we are simply servants, following orders.

Acts: The Church is Born

Session 11: Paul on Trial

Just for Kids

Get a dictionary and look up the word "appeal." What did Paul mean when he said, "I appeal to Caesar?"

Who was Caesar?

What would happen to Paul if he went to Jerusalem to stand trial?

Why did Paul appeal to Caesar?

Read Romans 15:24. When Paul wanted to go to Rome, do you think he had in mind being a prisoner?

Have you ever had plans that didn't work out the way you wanted them to? How did you feel?

We need to remember that God is in control of all things. Even if things don't work out the way we expect them to, we can always trust that God has something better in store for us.

Acts: The Church is Born

Session 11: Paul on Trial

Lesson 4

Acts 25:13-27

Read the following commentary for context:

> Herod Agrippa II, called simply Agrippa in Scripture, was the son of the Herod in Acts 12. Bernice and Drusilla (24:24) were his sisters. Since he was young when his father died, he did not receive his father's realm. But as the years passed he received one part and eventually the rest. He had a long reign, from a.d. 50 until about a.d. 100. His incestuous relations with his sister Bernice became a subject of gossip as far away as Rome. (Only Reference, Acts 25, 26.)[4]

Given the article above regarding Agrippa II, and understanding that Festus was the new kid on the block, what political dynamics must have been at play when Paul was brought before Agrippa?

What was Festus' assessment of Paul and the case brought against him?

Before Agrippa

The readings for today and tomorrow are actually a climax for the book of Acts. It is in this scene that we see Paul come before the "king of the Jews" and present his testimony and the gospel message clearly and boldly. During this whole week, Luke is demonstrating the legal innocence of the Gospel and the theological consistency between the Gospel and the Old Testament. Paul has stood before two Roman governors and has been proven innocent. Now, in the great climax, Paul stands before none other than Herod Agrippa II and his incestuous sister/wife, Bernice.

Tomorrow we will discuss Paul's message, so, for today, let's focus on Agrippa himself. In order to understand the impact and importance of this meeting we must realize the history that Agrippa brings to the table and its impact on the Gospel story. Agrippa's Great-Grandfather was the Herod who reigned during Jesus' birth, was visited by the Magi from the East, and ordered the boys of Bethlehem to be massacred. Agrippa's great uncle was the Herod, known as Antipas, who Jesus called a "fox" that had John the Baptist beheaded. Agrippa II's father, Agrippa, was the Herod that had James, the brother of John, killed and Peter imprisoned. It was he who died and became worm food. Now, bearing all this heritage of anti-Jesus baggage with him, Agrippa II, stands in judgment over Paul, the ambassador of Jesus.

Agrippa was the caricature of what God's people had become. He was a sell-out to Rome. He was messing around in an incestuous relationship with his sister. He was the inheritor of a great deal of distorted sin. Yet, he was the political "ruler" of his people. It is sad, but appropriate, to see Agrippa as the picture of what Israel had become. The prophets throughout the Old Testament were constantly warning the people to not mess around with the foreign gods or follow their ways. When they did, it led them only to destruction. Agrippa is the stark reminder that Israel, as a political entity, was on its way to disaster. How ironic that one of the greatest men in the Kingdom of God was standing in chains and the simple smock of a prisoner while the fool was clothed in riches and entered in great pomp. Jesus said, "If you want to be great in the Kingdom of Heaven, you will become last." And, "the first shall become last."

Acts: The Church is Born

Session 11: Paul on Trial

Just for Kids

Draw a family tree of Herod Agrippa II based on the following paragraph:

In order to understand the impact and importance of this meeting we must realize the history that Agrippa brings to the table and its impact on the Gospel story. Agrippa's Great-Grandfather was the Herod who reined during Jesus' birth, was visited by the Magi from the East, and ordered the boys of Bethlehem to be massacred. Agrippa's Great Uncle was the Herod, known as Antipas, who Jesus called a 'fox' that had John the Baptist beheaded. Agrippa II's father, Agrippa, was the Herod that had James, the brother of John, killed and Peter imprisoned. It was he who died and became worm food. Now, bearing all this heritage of anti-Jesus baggage with him, Agrippa II, stands in judgment over Paul, the ambassador of Jesus.

Based on this history, how do you think Agrippa felt about Paul and his message?

Tomorrow we will see what happens when Agrippa listens to Paul's message.

Acts: The Church is Born

Session 11: Paul on Trial

Lesson 5

Acts 26:1-32

How does Paul describe the hope that he has?

Describe Paul's mission before he encountered Jesus. Where did he go?

Why was it important that Paul mention that the voice was speaking Aramaic?

Compare and contrast Paul's testimony in this passage with his testimony in 22:1-21.

What is Paul's mission as it is outlined in vv. 17-18?

What was the heart of Paul's message? (v. 20)

What is the bottom line of Paul's message? (v. 23)

How does Festus respond to Paul?

Describe the interchange between Paul and Agrippa in your own words.

What was Agrippa's final assessment of Paul's situation?

Acts: The Church is Born

Session 11: Paul on Trial

Before Agrippa p.2

This is the last time we get to hear Paul's testimony. It would be a good study to compare and contrast each time Paul gives his testimony and notice how he modifies it each time depending upon his audience.

This time, as he presents his story to the Jewish king, he makes some important points.

1. **The hope has never changed.** All of Israel has been built upon the simple promise that God made to the patriarchs. God promised to Abraham that God would make him into a great nation and that, through him, all nations would be blessed. God also promised to David that there would be an eternal King on the throne. That has been their hope, and now, Paul is simply declaring that that hope has been fulfilled in Jesus Christ. This is an important point because we must never slip into an anti-Semitic (anti-Jewish) mentality as Christians. God is not against the Jews. We, as Christians, are actually wild branches that have been grafted into the vine of Israel through the person of Jesus. God did not change God's plan with Jesus, God simply fulfilled God's original promise.

2. **Paul's method and style didn't change, simply his mission did.** Notice, in v. 11, that Paul said he "went from one synagogue to another." Isn't that exactly what he did after he followed Jesus? On his missionary journeys he moved with zeal from one synagogue to another, reasoning from the scriptures that Jesus was the Messiah. Perhaps we can make this reasonable jump and assumption. Paul was born with a certain style and personality. He was an activist who took charge of the situation and moved out. That is how he would naturally operate regardless of his belief system or motivation. When he met Jesus, his perspective changed, but his style did not. That is how God works. God created us to be who we are, naturally. Unfortunately, when we are apart from God, we use those traits and tendencies for very destructive things. When God gets a hold of us God breaks us and brings our natural design into conformity with God's will. Paul didn't stop being a zealous go-getter for God, he simply became a broken and humble vessel to be used in the manner and place that God desired.

3. **Everything centers around the person of the resurrected Jesus.** It is vital that we never lose sight of the fact that Paul was not converted to a new religion. Paul entered into a relationship with a risen Lord. He was sent to be a servant and a witness to this reality. The world does not need a new set of rules and regulations and religious hierarchy. The world needs transparent witnesses to the reality of the risen Jesus; plain and simple.

4. **It's a matter of change.** Note the process that Jesus said would happen when people met him through Paul's ministry.

> **Open their eyes.** This is knowledge and paradigm shift. It comes through teaching.
>
> **Turn from darkness to light.** This is what "repentance" means. When people see the reality that they have been blinded by satan they will begin the process of moving out of his kingdom and into the Kingdom of God.
>
> **Receive forgiveness.** It is important to note that they do not earn forgiveness...they receive it. God is offering forgiveness to everyone. It is only when we are no longer blind that we can receive it.
>
> **A place among the sanctified.** To be sanctified is to be "holy"; to be washed clean. To have faith is to trust. When our trust is in the risen Jesus, we will be set free from our bondage of sin and washed clean. That is the Good News!

5. **The hope has never changed.** Paul ends where he began. Moses and the prophets all said that this would happen – that the Messiah would suffer, die, and rise again. So, Paul is simply being a fulfilled Pharisee, living in the realized hope of the resurrected Jesus.

Where is your hope today? Do you live like you know the risen Jesus and will be in eternity with him, or do you get bogged down in the muck and mire of every day distractions?

Acts: The Church is Born

Session 11: Paul on Trial

Just for Kids

Have you ever noticed that people are very different from each other? Each individual has certain strengths or things that they are good at or ways that they behave. Spend some time talking about each member of your family and the strengths that they have in their personality.

In the study today, we hear Paul's testimony again. Paul said that before he met Jesus, when he was really against the followers of Jesus, he went from synagogue to synagogue, arresting Jesus' disciples. Isn't it interesting that after he met Jesus he did the same thing? Instead of going from synagogue to synagogue arresting people, though, he went there to reason from the scriptures to show them that Jesus is the Messiah that the Old Testament predicted.

If you have given your life to Jesus, he wants to use your strengths to use for his Kingdom. Spend some time talking about how you think God could use your strengths for God's Kingdom.

(Footnotes)

[1] Wood, D. R. W. (1996). New Bible dictionary (3rd ed. /) (Page 367). Leicester, England; Downers Grove, Ill.: InterVarsity Press.

[2] Achtemeier, P. J. (1985). Harper's Bible dictionary. Includes index. (1st ed.) (Page 229). San Francisco: Harper & Row.

[3] Wood, D. R. W. (1996). New Bible dictionary (3rd ed. /) (Page 367). Leicester, England; Downers Grove, Ill.: InterVarsity Press.

[4] King James Version study Bible. 1997, c1988 (electronic ed.) (Ac 26:10). Nashville: Thomas Nelson.

Acts: The Church is Born

Session 12: On to Rome

Introduction

The ship has landed. The tree has spread its branches wide across the Empire of Rome and has cast its soothing shade over a sin-scorched earth. In these last two chapters of Acts, we see Paul make his final journey. He had planned to travel to Rome on his way to Spain as a missionary. But, as is often the case when you are a servant of God, he had his plans slightly skewed. Paul had the right destination in mind; he just got the means of transportation wrong. Instead of entering Rome as a courageous missionary, he came as a broken and humble prisoner.

Throughout these two chapters, we see that Luke draws one final, poetic portrait of the Kingdom of God as he contrasts the island of Malta with the city of Rome. Where does the Kingdom manifest? Is it in the cultural capital of the world where the most power and influence can be wielded by strategic evangelistic thinkers? No. It is poured out on a little island, by a broken prisoner, in the middle of the ocean. In Rome ,the Kingdom is lukewarmly received and the story ends in a somewhat anti-climactic tone. Luke never fails to point out the irony of the Kingdom of God. Jesus and his followers are not of this world. We are pilgrims, passing through, leaving in our wake the opening and invitation to enter into the eternal Kingdom of God and enjoy life to the fullest.

Acts: The Church is Born

Session 12: On to Rome

Lesson 1

Acts 27:1-12

Who were Paul's traveling companions?

Read the following passages.

    Acts 19:29

    Acts 20:4

    Colossians 4:10

    Philemon 24

Who was Aristarchus?

What cities of importance to Paul were located in Cilicia and Pamphylia? (Read Acts 21:39 and Acts 13:13ff to refresh your memory)

What was Paul's warning?

Read the following commentary:

Pagans undertaking sea voyages always sacrificed to the gods and sought their protection. Bad omens, astrological interpretations or dreams sometimes prevented a ship from sailing if they were taken seriously. Before going to war Romans would check the entrails of animals, the flight of birds and other forms of divination; religious advice was always important to those contemplating a potentially risky venture. Paul would sound to them like the kind of seer who could predict the future without divination. Unlike Greeks, Romans respected divination more than this kind of prophecy.[1]

In light of the above commentary, how do you think the Romans viewed Paul's words?

To whom did the centurion listen? Why?

How would you describe this leg of the journey? Was it easy or difficult?

Acts: The Church is Born

Session 12: On to Rome

A New Kind of Voyage

Today let's spend some time trying to crawl into the skin of Paul. Here it has been over two years since he first brought his love gift to Jerusalem, only to be reciprocated by death threats and false accusations. The time must have passed slowly as he sat in Caesarean captivity at the hands of the greedy Felix. Now, after his appeal to Caesar that saved him from the death trap that the Jewish leaders had laid for him in Jerusalem, Paul was about to embark on his next journey. Before, his journeys began in the company of his close friends, in the anticipation of great ministry, and under the commissioning hands of the elders of Antioch. Not this time. Now he sat fettered to a string of convicts, many of whom were most likely murderers that were headed to be lion food and entertainment for the blood-sport of the Coliseum. It is hard to imagine what must have been going through his mind as they set sail that day.

They say that, just before death, your life passes before your eyes. Perhaps this is the tone that Luke wanted to set as Paul passed by the shores of Cilicia and Pamphylia. The Cilician shores flooded in waves of childhood memories as Paul had grown up in Tarsus of Cilicia. Here he was the Jewish boy who dreamed of studying in Jerusalem. In Pamphylia he remembered that first journey. This region was his doorway into Galatia. It was here that he traveled through Antioch Pisidia, Iconium, Lystra, and Derbe. He was worshipped as a god, and stoned as a heretic. He met Timothy here, and planted many churches.

As the prison voyage continued, he passed along the Southern shore of Asia. Ah, Asia, with Ephesus at its heart. Ephesus was the place where God had shown up in a mighty way and performed great miracles through Paul. Many great churches had been planted from that Asian hub.

Now with Luke and Aristarchus by his side, Paul's journey headed south toward Crete. It was getting late in the year and was well past sailing season. As the winds grew stronger and the waves grew more violent, Paul cautioned the Romans that this trip would not end well if they did not set port in Crete. But, to no avail, the head-strong, money-conscious, practical thinking Romans paid him no heed and headed into disaster.

There are two simple observations and take homes for today.

1. **Even as a prisoner, Paul was in tune with God.** Had Paul not been walking in the Spirit, he would not have heard God's warning and spoken the prophetic word to the Romans. No matter what our circumstances may be, we must always stay in step with the Spirit, because he could use us at any time. You never know.

2. **The greed of the Romans kept them from being able to hear the voice of truth.** The Romans were not willing to hear the voice of a Hebrew prophet. If there were no animal entrails or incantations involved in the prophetic word, then they would rather listen to their own instincts than to the words of Paul. Tomorrow we will see where that kind of thinking and spiritual blindness ended up.

Just for Kids

Draw a picture of Paul sitting on a boat, in chains, between some criminals. Now draw two thought bubbles. On one side write what you think Paul might have been thinking at this point in his life. On the other side either write or draw a picture of God bringing comfort and reassurance to Paul.

It is important for us to always remember that, no matter how bad things may get, God is always with us.

Acts: The Church is Born

Session 12: On to Rome

Lesson 2

Acts 27:13-44

What did the crew do in order to try to survive the storm?

What was the attitude of the crew after a few days of storm?

What message did Paul give the crew?

Now that Paul had spoken his second prophetic word (see yesterday's reading for the first) how do you think the Romans felt about his words now?

Based upon the soldiers' response in v. 32, how do you think the Romans viewed Paul at this point?

In what way did Paul bring comfort and hope to the crew?

Based upon the centurion's actions in v. 43, how do you think he viewed Paul at this point?

A Shepherd at Sea

Do you know what the test is to see if you are a leader? Look to see if anyone is following you. Many times people think that being a great leader in God's church requires a position, or a title, or maybe even an office with a window, or a television show. With the position comes the power and the position from which people will be able to hear your words and follow your leadership. In this story, we see that Paul truly was an anointed leader for God and demonstrated that leadership doesn't need any of those things. Think about it. Paul was a prisoner. He was shackled together with common criminals. He was riding on a grain barge between a low-life cargo captain and a common centurion. There was nothing glamorous here. Paul was at the bottom of the socio-economic ladder.

And yet, none of that mattered to him. Throughout this story we can see that two things were true about Paul. The first is that he always focused on his relationship with God and remained in the Spirit at all times, regardless of his circumstances. We know this is true because he received yet another message from God. This time God even sent an angel to assure him that all would be well. The second thing about Paul was that he exercised his gifts regardless of his situation. Paul was an apostle, a leader, and a shepherd. Even with chains on his hands and feet, Paul took charge of the situation. He had compassion on the men aboard this ship. He spoke boldly and instilled courage into the hearts of men who had given up hope. Here was a Jewish rabbi standing in the middle of seasoned sea-farers. While sailors had given up, the rabbi stood strong.

In many ways this story parallels the period of Jesus' life between the feeding of the 5,000 and the feeding of the 4,000. In between those two events Jesus walked out across a stormy lake and brought courage and hope to his bewildered disciples. In that act, Jesus demonstrated that he had power over the forces of nature and was truly the King of the entire universe. He could provide bread for his people, empower them to walk on the water, and he could calm the storm. Now Paul, the disciple of the risen Jesus, showed Jesus-like courage in the face of the storm. What gave him this courage? It was the promise. Jesus had promised him that he and the whole crew would not perish. Paul's faith in the promise gave him the ability to see above the storm and have enough composure to not only encourage 276 frightened men, but also to bake bread for them and share table

Acts: The Church is Born

Session 12: On to Rome

fellowship. Imagine that! Most of us would have been freaking out and wondering why God had abandoned us.

Here a thought for today. Jesus has given us a promise. He promised that if we trust him he would prepare a place for us in the Father's presence. He told us that he would give us the Holy Spirit to teach us, comfort us, convict us, and encourage us. He promised that he would protect us from the evil one. We live in a life full of storms. We are daily pounded by gale-strength winds that oppose our Kingdom worldview. We are plagued by the enemy's attempts to riddle us with fear, doubt, anxiety, anger, and bitterness. Yet, in the face of all of that, we, too, can rise above it and cling to the promise. God does love us. Jesus has made a way for us to know the abundant life of relationship with God. The Holy Spirit has been placed in our lives as the deposit, guaranteeing our eternal life. We do not have to be waylaid by the storm. We can rise above it and have the strength to speak God's words to the people around us, comfort them, and break bread with them while the wind whips past us.

Just for Kids

Today is the big storm. Have some fun and act out the scene of the storm. Make a boat out of chairs. Flash the lights for lightning.

Read the story carefully and see what kind of dialogue happens between Paul and the soldiers.

Why do you think Paul was so courageous and confident during this storm?

Have you ever had a time when you were really scared? Think back to that time and try to see yourself being confident like Paul.

The next time a big "storm" comes in your life, remember that you don't have to be afraid. God is with you.

Acts: The Church is Born

Session 12: On to Rome

Lesson 3

Acts 28:1-10

Read the following article excerpt about Malta:

> Malta had been occupied from the 7th century BC by Phoenicians. The name itself means 'refuge' in that language (J. R. Harris, ExpT 21, 1909–10, p. 18). Later, Sicilian Greeks also came; there are bilingual inscriptions of the 1st century AD on the island. In 218 BC the island passed from Carthaginian to Roman control (Livy, 21. 51), later gaining the 'civitas'. Its inhabitants were barbaroi (28:2, 4) only in the sense of not speaking Greek. Luke may refer to one of their gods in v. 4 as Dikē (Justice). Publius, 'the chief man' (v. 7), probably served under the propraetor of Sicily. His title (Gk. prōtos) is attested by inscriptions (CIG, 14. 601; CIL, 10. 7495).[2]

What was the first assumption made about Paul after the viper incident? Why?

How did their opinion change? Why?

What did Paul do for the people?

Read Mark 16:15-18. What correlation do you see between Paul's Malta experience and these words of Jesus?

How were the "prisoners" treated on Malta? Why?

How long did they stay on Malta? (read v. 11)

A Picture of the Kingdom

As we read today's section we move into the final chapter of Acts. Remember, Luke is a brilliant author and does not just slap down narrative details for no particular reason. Everything has a purpose. In this final chapter, Luke is drawing one final picture of the Kingdom of God on earth. Luke started this epic saga way back in the first chapter of his Gospel when the angel appeared to Zechariah and to Mary. There was an invasion about to happen. God was bringing about the fulfillment of prophecy and the one true King of Israel was about to come to turn the world upside down and establish his rightful Kingdom on the earth. Jesus came in humility and in power. He cast out demons, he healed the sick, and he taught with authority. He conquered the forces of darkness and broke the chains of death from the world and ushered in the Kingdom of God. Then he commissioned his disciples to go and do the same. He gave them authority and power to be the ambassadors and the seed planters of his eternal Kingdom wherever they went. In this story Luke describes to us in eloquent terms what the Kingdom is truly all about. Here are some observations that will help us understand the Kingdom of God.

1. **It is not of this world and is impervious to fleshly circumstances.** Paul didn't come to Malta as a fully supported missionary with a ready-made plan for evangelizing the island. He dragged his soggy rear out of the ocean bearing the marks of a common criminal for crying out loud. Yet, in God's plan that didn't matter. Paul was a missionary. That IS what God made him to be. It wasn't a POSITION that he filled, it was the way he WAS.

2. **The Kingdom is often misperceived at first.** When the islanders saw the viper bite Paul they automatically assumed he was a criminal and that their god – Justice – was executing him. When Paul didn't die, or even get sick, they then assumed that Paul was a god. In both cases they were wrong. They were looking through their native worldview lenses and trying to interpret the truth of God's Kingdom through their native grid of understanding. It is only natural for people to do this, for it is nearly impossible to see things outside of our own worldview. It is not until our eyes are opened and we are willing to climb out of our own perspective that

Acts: The Church is Born

Session 12: On to Rome

we can begin to see the truth. The truth was that Paul was neither a criminal nor a god. He was simply a servant of Jesus who was living in the power of Jesus' promise and purpose.

3. **It's about healing.** What did Jesus do when he came to a new region? He healed people. What did Peter, Philip, Paul, Barnabas, and Silas do when they came to a new region? Note: What did they do especially when they came to a new region that did not have a synagogue in which they could reason from the scripture? They healed people. They delivered people from the sickness and death that plagued them as a result of their blindness and the lost condition of the world. The Kingdom of God is about new life. It is about reconciliation to the original design that God had for us in the Garden. Jesus came to give us life and to give it to the full. So, here is Paul, a prisoner, living in what would be by fleshly standards, the worst possible position in life, oozing out the Kingdom of God on a small island 100 km south of Sicily. It wasn't in Rome. It wasn't in Jerusalem. It wasn't through a mega-powered, satellite driven program. It was a prisoner who was walking in the Spirit, overflowing the Kingdom on a bunch of simple islanders out in the middle of the ocean. You've got to love it. Now, let's live it.

Just for Kids

What did the islanders think would happen to Paul when the snake bit him? Why?

What did the islanders think about Paul after he was unaffected by the snake? Why?

Was either of these ideas about Paul correct? Why?

What was Paul?

How did Paul demonstrate the power of God on the island?

Do you know anyone that is sick? Spend some time praying for that person and ask God to show you ways that you could bring comfort and healing to their life.

Acts: The Church is Born

Session 12: On to Rome

Lesson 4

Acts 28:11-31

Read this commentary:

> The seas opened as early as February 8 or as late as March 10, depending on the weather; in the year in view here they seem to open toward the earlier date. On Alexandrian ships see comment on 27:6; like most ships, this one would have harbored on the other side of the island. Ships were named for their patron deity (e.g., "the Isis") in whose protection they trusted and whose image was used as the ship's figurehead. The Dioscuri (Castor and Pollux, twin heroes, sons of Zeus who had been deified) were considered special protectors of ships, on whom one might call in a storm.[3]

In light of the above information regarding the Greek gods, do you see any possible irony in Luke's writing?

Summarize Paul's opening statement to the Jews.

How was Paul received by the Jews in Rome?

What was the heart of Paul's message? (v. 23)

What was Paul's concluding remarks regarding the Jews and his ministry?

What portrait is painted of Paul as the book of Acts ends?

An Unusual Ending

Yesterday we saw how Luke painted a beautiful portrait of the Kingdom of God pouring out on the little island of Malta. Today, in this final scene in the book of Acts, we see that Luke draws a stark contrast to yesterday's portrait. In many ways this scene is surprisingly anti-climactic. It seems as if Paul's life has been building up to this moment. He's had a big showdown with the Jews in Jerusalem where they want to kill him. They forced his hand and he appealed to Caesar. Now he has fought against a vicious storm, the chains of bondage, and a poisonous viper to come to this final moment. Here he will stand before Caesar and see himself and the Kingdom vindicated before the world.

Nope.

That's not how it went down at all. Here is a dialogue that will paraphrase the tone and possible intent of this scene.

Paul: Hello, Rome. I'm here. Hello Jewish leaders. I know you probably want to kill me. I'm sure the HQ in Jerusalem has sent their secret orders to slit my throat in the night.

Jews: Huh? We don't know what you're talking about. We haven't heard anything about you from Jerusalem. In fact, you seem like a pretty nice guy to us. Why would we want to hurt you?

Paul: Oh. OK. In that case let me tell you why I'm here. I have come to tell you that the Kingdom of God has come just the way God promised throughout the scriptures. The Kingdom has come and his name is Jesus. Jesus died and rose from the dead and now he offers the Kingdom to anyone who wants to trust him. It's open to Jew and Gentile alike. It's that simple.

Jews: Oh, that's interesting. Some of us like it. We're in. Some of us don't, so we'll be leaving now. Hope the whole house arrest thing works out for you, Paul.

Paul: God said you wouldn't believe. That's why it is open to the Gentiles.

Oh, by the way, do I have a court date yet?

Roman: No. we're not even sure if you can get in to see the emperor. Enjoy the house arrest.

So, there you have it. No big court scene. No big mob of angry Jews. It's just Paul living in a rented house, under house arrest, teaching more disciples – Jew and Gentile – about the Kingdom of God. Then it ends.

Acts: The Church is Born

Session 12: On to Rome

Here are some lessons we should learn from this:

1. **The Kingdom of God isn't about big dramatic endings, it's about everyday life.**
2. **The Kingdom of God is for everyone, anywhere.** It can be in the Temple at Jerusalem, it can be in the lecture hall at Ephesus, it can be on the beach of Malta, or in a rented house in the capital of the Empire.
3. **The Kingdom of God is all about the risen Jesus.** Here is the main point of Luke/Acts. The Kingdom begins and ends with the risen Jesus. He is the King. It's about him. It's not about Peter. It's not about Paul. It's about Jesus. Peter and Paul, and we, are simply servants of the King. Never forget that.

The story isn't over. Luke intentionally left the story hanging because he knew it wasn't over. Paul was eventually released. He did make it on to Spain. Then he was arrested again and executed in Rome. But that didn't end the story. The book of Acts, the spreading of the great tree called the Kingdom of God is a story that lives forever. It lives on with you and with me. We are writing the 29th chapter of Acts right now, as we live, act, and speak in our everyday lives. How's the story so far?

Just for Kids

We've come to the end of Acts. Throughout the whole story we have watched and listened as the apostles spread the Good News of the Kingdom of God and the resurrected Jesus to the world.

There are two main points about the Kingdom that we must remember from Acts:

1. It is all about Jesus. He is the King and everything is done for him.

2. Everyone is welcome. It doesn't matter who you are or what you have done, God wants everyone, everywhere to know God.

Draw a picture that shows the Kingdom of God and illustrates these two main points.

Acts: The Church is Born

Session 12: On to Rome

Lesson 5

Acts 29

Yesterday we said that we are living the 29th chapter of Acts. We are the church. We are the inheritors of the Kingdom that the Father gave to Jesus and we live in it through the power of the Holy Spirit. We look to Peter and Paul as examples and pioneers of the Kingdom Way and how to spread the Good News and live in the Kingdom each day. The real question for us, as we conclude this study, is, "How well are we living in the everyday life of the Kingdom?"

Spend some time today looking over your notes for the last 12 weeks of study. As you read through this outline, make notes regarding what you learned and how God challenged you in this study.

The church is born in Jerusalem (1-2)

The church experiences opposition in Jerusalem (3-7)

Abraham's family (Hebraic Jews, Grecian Jews, and Samaritans) is reconciled through the Holy Spirit. (8-12)

The Church spreads to the Gentiles

Galatia (13-15)

Macedonia and Greece (16-18)

Ephesus and the collection (19-20)

Paul the Prisoner (21-28)

Ask God to show you the ways in which you and your church can grow to become more like our "founding fathers" that were described in the book of Acts.

Just for Kids

The kids can do the same exercise as the adults today. Have fun spending time as a family revisiting the big picture of Acts. Perhaps you could walk through all of the weekly illustrations and recap the story.

(Footnotes)

[1] Keener, C. S. (1993). The IVP Bible background commentary: New Testament (Ac 27:10). Downers Grove, Ill.: InterVarsity Press.

[2] Wood, D. R. W. (1996). *New Bible dictionary* (3rd ed. /) (Page 720). Leicester, England; Downers Grove, Ill.: InterVarsity Press.

[3] Keener, C. S. (1993). *The IVP Bible background commentary : New Testament* (Ac 28:11). Downers Grove, Ill.: InterVarsity Press.